# THE FUTURE OF INTELLECTUALS
# AND THE RISE OF THE NEW CLASS

This Volume Is Part of a Trilogy

THE DARK SIDE OF THE DIALECTIC

*by Alvin W. Gouldner*

VOLUME ONE

The Dialectic of Ideology and Technology

VOLUME TWO

The Future of Intellectuals and the Rise of the New Class

VOLUME THREE

The Two Marxisms: Contradictions and Anomalies
in the Development of Theory

OTHER BOOKS BY ALVIN W. GOULDNER

Studies in Leadership: Leadership and Democratic Action

Patterns of Industrial Bureaucracy

Wildcat Strike

Emile Durkheims's Socialism and Saint-Simon

Notes on Technology and the Moral Order
(with Richard A. Peterson)

Enter Plato: The Origins of
Western Social Theory in Ancient Greece

The Coming Crisis of Western Sociology

For Sociology: Renewal and Critique in Sociology Today

# The Future of Intellectuals and the Rise of the New Class

A Frame of Reference, Theses,
Conjectures, Arguments, and an
Historical Perspective on the Role of
Intellectuals and Intelligentsia
in the International Class Contest
of the Modern Era

## ALVIN W. GOULDNER

*105078*

OXFORD UNIVERSITY PRESS
New York     Toronto

Copyright© 1979 by Alvin W. Gouldner

First published by The Seabury Press as A Continuum Book, New York, 1979
First issued as an Oxford University Press paperback, New York, 1982,
    by arrangement with The Continuum Publishing Corporation

Library of Congress Cataloging in Publication Data

Gouldner, Alvin Ward, 1920—
The future of intellectuals and the rise of the new class.

    Bibliography.
    Includes index.
    1. Intellectuals.    2. Social classes.    3. Sociolinguistics
    I. Title.
HM213.G68    301.44′5    78-24442
ISBN 0-19-503065-6 (pbk.)

This printing (last digit):  9 8 7 6 5 4 3 2 1

Printed in the United States of America

# CONTENTS

# ACKNOWLEDGMENTS

During the summer of 1977 I directed a seminar at Washington University, sponsored by the National Endowment for the Humanities, at which I discussed the full set of theses on the New Class presented here with some revisions. The scholars who attended this seminar, and for whose criticisms I am thankful, were: Andrew Arato, Rod Camp, Richard Colvard, Cornelis Disco, Geoffrey Fox, Suren Gupta, Joseph Healey, Will Keim, Khalil Nakhleh, John Neumaier, Roger Newcomb, and Edward Price. I especially appreciated the opportunity to discuss the theses with colleagues at the University of Zagreb; the University of Copenhagen; the Institute for Higher Studies, Vienna; and the School of Economics at Stockholm, while lecturing in Europe during the fall of 1977. I am particularly indebted for the assistance of Robert McAulay, Judy Green, and Janet Walker Gouldner. Errors and lacunae still remaining in this work are entirely my own.

Be robbers and conquerors, as long as you cannot be
rulers and owners, you lovers of knowledge! Soon the
age will be past when you could be satisfied to live
like shy deer, hidden in the woods! At long last the
pursuit of knowledge will reach out for its due:
it will want to *rule* and *own;* and you with it!

Nietzsche, *The Gay Science*

Discontent among the lower classes may produce a serious
illness for which we have remedies, but discontent among the
educated minority leads to a chronic disease whose diagnosis
is difficult and cure protracted.

Otto von Bismarck, *Werke*, XIII, 563

# INTRODUCTION

In all countries that have in the twentieth century become part of the emerging world socio-economic order, a New Class composed of intellectuals and technical intelligentsia—not the same—enter into contention with the groups already in control of the society's economy, whether these are businessmen or party leaders. A new contest of classes and a new class system is slowly arising in the third world of developing nations, in the second world of the USSR and its client states, and in the first world of late capitalism of North America, Western Europe, and Japan.

The early historical evolution of the New Class in Western Europe, its emergence into the public sphere as a structurally differentiated and (relatively) autonomous social stratum, may be defined in terms of certain critical episodes. What follows is only a synoptic inventory of *some* episodes decisive in the formation of the New Class.

1. A process of secularization in which most intelligentsia are no longer trained by, living within, and subject to close supervision by a churchly organization, and thus separated from the everyday life of society.[1]

    Secularization is important because it de-sacralizes authority-claims and facilitates challenges to definitions of social reality made by traditional authorities linked to the church. Secularization is important also because it is an infra-structure on which there develops the modern grammar of rationality, or culture of critical discourse, with its characteristic stress on self-groundedness—in Martin Heidegger's sense of the "mathematical project."[2]

2. A second episode in the emergence of the New Class is the rise of diverse vernacular languages, the corresponding decline of Latin as the language of intellectuals, and especially of their scholarly production. Latin becomes a ritual, rather than a technical language. This development further dissolves the membrane be-

tween everyday life and the intellectuals—whether clerical or secular.

3. There is a breakdown of the feudal and old regime system of personalized *patronage* relations between the old hegemonic elite and individual members of the New Class as cultural producers, and

4. A corresponding growth of an anonymous *market* for the products and services of the New Class, thus allowing them to make an independent living apart from close supervision and *personalized controls by patrons*. Along with secularization, this means that the residence and work of intellectuals are both now less closely supervised by others.

   They may now more readily take personal initiatives in the public, political sphere, while also having a "private" life.

5. The character and development of the emerging New Class also depended importantly on the multi-national structure of European polities. That Europe was not a single empire with a central authority able to impose a single set of norms throughout its territory, but a system of competing and autonomous states with diverse cultures and religions, meant that dissenting intellectuals, scientists, and divines could and did protect their own intellectual innovations by migrating from their home country when conditions there grew insupportable and sojourning in foreign lands. Even the enforced travel of exiled intellectuals also enabled them to enter into a European-wide communication network. In an article (as yet unpublished), Robert Wuthnow has suggested that their often extensive travel led many intellectuals to share a cosmopolitan identity transcending national limits and enhancing their autonomy from local elites.

6. A sixth episode in the formation of the New Class is the waning of the extended, patriarchical family system and its replacement by the smaller, nuclear family. As middle class women become educated and emancipated, they may increasingly challenge paternal authority and side with their children in resisting it. With declining paternal authority and growing maternal influence, the autonomy strivings of children are now more difficult to repress; hostility and rebellion against paternal authority can become more overt. There is, correspondingly, increasing difficulty experienced by paternal authority in imposing and reproducing its social values and political ideologies in their children.

7. Following the French Revolution, there is in many parts of Europe, especially France and Germany, a profound reformation and extension of *public, non*-church controlled, (relatively more) *multi-class* education, at the lower levels as well as at the college, polytechnical, and university levels. On the one hand, higher education in the public school becomes the institutional basis for the *mass* production of the New Class of intelligentsia and intellectuals. On the other hand, the expansion of primary and secondary public school teachers greatly increases the jobs available to the New Class.

As teachers, intellectuals come to be defined, and to define themselves, as responsible for and "representative" of society as a *whole*,[3] rather than as having allegiance to the class interests of their students or their parents. As teachers, they are not defined as having an *obligation* to reproduce parental values in their children. Public teachers supersede private tutors.

8. The new structurally differentiated educational system is increasingly insulated from the family system, becoming an important source of values among students divergent from those of their families. The socialization of the young by their families is now mediated by a *semi*-autonomous group of teachers.

9. While growing public education limits family influence on education, it also increases the influence of the state on education. The public educational system thus becomes a major *cosmopolitanizing* influence on its students, with a corresponding distancing from *localistic* interests and values.

10. Again, the new school system becomes a major setting for the intensive linguistic conversion of students from casual to reflexive speech, or (in Basil Bernstein's terms) from "restricted" linguistic codes to "elaborated" linguistic codes,[4] to a culture of discourse in which claims and assertions may *not* be justified by reference to the speaker's social status. This has the profound consequence of making all *authority-referring* claims potentially problematic.

11. This new culture of discourse often diverges from assumptions fundamental to everyday life, tending to put them into question even when they are linked to the upper classes. These school-inculcated modes of speech are, also, (relatively) situation-free language variants. Their situation-freeness is further heightened by the "communications revolution" in general, and by the development of printing technology, in particular. With the spread of

printed materials, definitions of social reality available to intellectuals may now derive increasingly from *distant* persons, from groups geographically, culturally, and historically distant and even from dead persons, and may therefore diverge greatly from any local environment in which they are received. Definitions of social reality made by local elites may now be invidiously contrasted (by intellectuals) with definitions made in other places and times.

12. With the spread of public schools, literacy spreads; humanistic intellectuals lose their exclusiveness and privileged market position, and now experience a status disparity between their "high" culture, as they see it, and their lower deference, repute, income and social power. The social position of humanistic intellectuals, *particularly in a technocratic and industrial society*, becomes more marginal and alienated than that of the technical intelligentsia. The New Class becomes internally differentiated.

13. Finally, a major episode in the emergence of the modern intelligentsia is the changing form of the revolutionary *organization*. Revolution itself becomes a technology to be pursued with "instrumental rationality." The revolutionary organization evolves from a ritualistic, oath-bound secret society into the modern "vanguard" party. When the *Communist Manifesto* remarks that Communists have nothing to hide,[5] it is exactly a proposed emergence into *public* life which is implied. The *Communist Manifesto* was written by Marx and Engels for the "League of Communists," which was born of the "League of the Just" which, in turn, was descended from the "League of Outlaws." This latter group of German emigrants in Paris had a pyramidal structure, made a sharp distinction between upper and lower members, blindfolded members during initiation ceremonies, used recognition signs and passwords, and bound members by an oath.[6] The vanguard organization, however, de-ritualizes participation and entails elements of both the "secret society" and of the public political party. In the vanguard organization, public refers to the public availability of the *doctrine* rather than the availability of the organization or its membership to public scrutiny. Here, to be "public" entails the organization's rejection of "secret doctrines" known only to an elite in the organization—as, for instance, Bakunin's doctrine of an elite dictatorship of anarchists.[7] The *modern* vanguard structure is first clearly encoded in

Lenin's *What Is to Be Done?* Here it is plainly held that the proletariat cannot develop a *socialist* consciousness by itself, but must secure this from a scientific theory developed by the intelligentsia.[8] The "vanguard" party expresses the *modernizing* and elite ambitions of the New Class as well as an effort to overcome its political limitations. Lenin's call for the development of "professional" revolutionaries, as the core of the vanguard, is a rhetoric carrying the tacit promise of a *career*-like life which invites young members of the New Class to "normalize" the revolutionary existence.

I shall return to and enlarge upon *some* of the critical episodes inventoried above. Above all, the attempt is to formulate a frame of reference within which the New Class can be situated, giving some indication of the intellectual work—theoretical and empirical—that needs to be done to understand the New Class as a world historical phenomenon. Rather than viewing the New Class as if it were composed just of technicians or engineers, the effort that follows moves toward a *general* theory of the New Class as encompassing *both* technical intelligentsia *and* intellectuals. Rather than focusing in a parochial way on the United States alone, my interest is in the New Class in *both* late capitalism and in the authoritarian state socialism of the USSR, without arguing or implying any more general "convergence" thesis. I shall suggest that the two most important theoretical foundations needed for a general theory of the New Class will be, first, a theory of its distinctive language behavior, its distinctive culture of discourse and, secondly, a general theory of capital within which the New Class's "human capital" or the old class's moneyed capital will be special cases.

The analysis to follow is grounded in what I can only call my own version of a "neo-Hegelian" sociology, a neo-Hegelianism which is a "left" but certainly not a "young" Hegelianism. It is *left* Hegelianism in that it holds that knowledge and knowledge systems are important in shaping social outcomes, but, far from seeing these as disembodied eternal essences, views them as the ideology of special social classes; and while ready to believe that knowledge is one of the best hopes we have for a humane social reconstruction, also sees our knowledge systems as historically shaped forces that embody limits and, indeed, pathologies.

Like any social object, the New Class can be defined in terms of both its imputed value or goodness and its imputed power.[9] In most cultural grammars, a "normal" social world is supposed to be one in which the powerful are good and the bad, weak. The temptation to see the world in this manner, to *normalize* it, is difficult to resist and one sees it at work in conceptions of the New Class. Thus Noam Chomsky sees the New Class as cynically corrupt *and* as weak, pliable tools of others. Conversely, John Galbraith views the technical intelligentsia as productively benign *and* as already dominant. Such judgments bear the impress (albeit in different directions) of normalizing tendencies and ought to be routinely suspect.

In contrast to such normalizing tendencies, a left Hegelian sociology accepts dissonance as part of reality. It does not assume that the strong are good or the bad, weak. It accepts the possibility that those who are becoming stronger—such as the New Class—and to whom the future *may* belong, are not always the better and may, indeed, be morally ambiguous.

There are, then, several distinguishable conceptions of the New Class:

1. *New Class as Benign Technocrats:* Here the New Class is viewed as a new historical elite already entrenched in institutional influence which it uses in benign ways for society; it is more or less inevitable and trustworthy: e.g., Galbraith,[10] Bell,[11] Berle and Means.[12]

   (*Sed contra:* This obscures the manner in which the New Class egoistically pursues its own special vested interests. Moreover, the power of the New Class today is scarcely entrenched. This view also ignores the limits on the rationality of the New Class.)

2. *New Class as Master Class:* Here the New Class is seen as another moment in a long-continuing circulation of historical elites, as a socialist intelligentsia that brings little new to the world and continues to exploit the rest of society as the old class had, but now uses education rather than money to exploit others: Bakunin,[13] Machajski.[14]

   (*Sed contra:* The New Class is more historically unique and discontinuous than this sees; while protecting its own special interests, it is not bound by the same *limits* as the old class and, at least transiently, contributes to collective needs.)

3. *New Class as Old Class Ally:* The New Class is here seen as a benign group of dedicated "professionals" who will uplift the old (moneyed) class from a venal group to a collectivity-oriented elite

and who, fusing with it, will forge a new, genteel elite continuous with but better than the past: Talcott Parsons. [15]

(*Sed contra:* Neither group is an especially morally bound agent; the old class is constrained to protect its profits, the New Class is cashing in on its education. Immersed in the present, this view misses the fact that each is ready to exploit the other, if need be, and shows little understanding of the profound (if different) limits imposed on the rationality and morality of each of these groups, and of the important tensions between them.)

4. *New Class as Servants of Power:* Here the New Class is viewed as subservient to the old (moneyed) class which is held to retain power much as it always did, and is simply using the New Class to maintain its domination of society: Noam Chomsky [16] and Maurice Zeitlin. [17]

   (*Sed contra:* This ignores the revolutionary history of the twentieth century in which radicalized elements of the New Class played a major leadership role in the key revolutions of our time. It greatly overemphasizes the common interests binding the New and old class, systematically missing the tensions between them; it ignores the fact that elimination of the old class is an historical option open to the New Class. This static conception underestimates the growth in the numbers and influence of the New Class. The view is also unexpectedly Marcusean in overstressing the prospects of old class continuity; it really sees the old class as having no effective opponents, either in the New Class or in the old adversary class, the proletariat. It thus ends as seeing even less social change in prospect than the Parsonian view (#3 above).

5. *New Class as Flawed Universal Class* (*my own view*): The New Class is elitist and self-seeking and uses its special knowledge to advance its own interests and power, and to control its own work situation. Yet the New Class may also be the best card that history has presently given us to play. The power of the New Class is growing. It is substantially more powerful and independent than Chomsky suggests, while still much less powerful than is suggested by Galbraith who seems to conflate present reality with future possibility. The power of this morally ambiguous New Class is on the ascendent and it holds a mortgage on at least *one* historical future.

In my own left Hegelian sociology, the New Class bearers of knowledge are seen as an embryonic new "universal class"—as the prefigured embodiment of such future as the working class still has. It is that part of the working class which will survive cybernation. At the same time, a left Hegelian sociology also insists that the New Class is profoundly flawed as a universal class. Moreover, the New Class is not some unified subject or a seamless whole; it, too, has its own internal contradictions. It is a class internally divided with tensions between (technical) intelligentsia and (humanistic) intellectuals. No celebration, mine is a critique of the New Class which does not view its growing power as inevitable, which sees it as morally ambivalent, embodying the collective interest but partially and transiently, while simultaneously cultivating its own guild advantage.

A *Terminological Note:* There are those who will be dismayed (and even enraged) that I call the New Class a "class," and who will insist that it is not really a class. If I may say so, my attitude toward this question is rather more Marxist than theirs. First, I remind them that, since Marx did little to define "class" formally and connotatively, I feel similarly free not to make a scholastic issue of this matter. Secondly: insofar as Marx has a clear concept of class it would appear to suggest that a class are those who have the same relationship to the means of production. In like manner, I, too, shall suggest that there are certain communalities in the New Class's relationship to the means of production and, in particular, to what I shall later call cultural capital or human capital. Third and finally, I remind those objecting to my use of "class" that the *Communist Manifesto* exhibits a not dissimilar usage. It holds that the term may be properly applied to such historically diverse groupings as slaves, serfs, journeymen or bourgeoisie, and clearly does not limit the term class to capitalist societies. If journeymen and plebians can be "classes," then surely intellectuals and intelligentsia can constitute a new "class." [18]

*As for "Theses":* I use this term in the standard way to mean the laying down of a position or the clarifying of essential contentions. The thrust of "theses" is toward an environing *discussion* and toward the compelling clarification of the speaker's *position*, so that it will not be misconstrued in the confusions of intellectual contention.

The "virtue" of a thesis, then, is its contribution to organizing discussion in an intellectual community by its pointed implications for certain intellectual traditions. The aim of theses is to muster clarity in *meaning*, which is necessarily antecedent to proof. But clarity is always dependent not on good but on *poor* vision; on blurring complex details in order to sight the main structure. The business of the theses that follow, then, is with the architecture of a discussion.

# Thesis One: Defects of the Marxist Scenario

The specter that had been said to be "haunting Europe" was an illusion. The claim that the central protagonists in modern class struggles were proletariat and capitalist class was an illusion. This was the Marxist scenario, and it was fundamentally inadequate.

*1.1 First Inadequacy:* The consequential revolutionary struggles of the twentieth century involved the *peasantry* as much or more than the proletariat. Clearly the case in the Chinese Revolution, it was also what happened in the Soviet Revolution. It was mostly the *peasantry* who, hating the war and yearning for land of their own, was the core of the Petrograd garrison which was the main fighting force that overthrew the Czarist government and who made the October Revolution. It was mostly the peasantry who, concerned to secure its new lands, that was the core of the Red Army which thwarted the forces of the counter-revolution. Indeed, the roots of Stalinism are in the deception and disappointment of the peasantry by a small urban elite aiming to control this vast rural majority.[19]

*1.2 Second Inadequacy:* The Marxist scenario of class struggle was never able to account for itself, for those who produced the scenario, for Marx and Engels themselves. Where did the *theorists* of this class struggle fit into the supposed cleavage between proletariat and capitalist class? When the question is raised, there is only embarrassment covered over by a silence. (One is not supposed to ask the television audience, "Where does the cameraman fit in?") Yes, there is a capitalist class; yes, a proletariat. And, yes, they often struggle with one another. But these have not been the decisive class struggles that, in the twentieth century, have produced revolutions that overturned states. And it is revolutions that *win state power and use it to effect a major property transfer—collectivization—that concern me here.*

# Thesis Two: Peasants and Vanguards

2.1   For such revolutions what was required was: (a) impairment of the old state's repressive apparatus, its armies and police, often through their military destruction by foreign armies; (b) waning legitimacy of the society's old ruling class, often due to inability to protect its own society from alien invasion and exploitation; (c) a rebellious peasantry, alienated partly because of its economic position; (d) alienation of intellectuals; (e) emergence of a new organization, the "vanguard party," which succeeds in identifying itself with the movement for national unity and with resistance to foreigners; and (f) where foreign states are reluctant or unable to help the old besieged regime.

2.2   Peasant alienation has nowhere in the modern period brought down a state and effected a major property transfer except in association with, and indeed, under the political and cultural tutelage of intellectuals.

2.3   The relationship of intellectuals with the peasantry and other masses is mediated by the new type of organization that understands itself as a "vanguard party." Without this organizational mediation, the intellectuals have no popular base and hence no power. As long as large numbers are not subject to political mobilization by intellectuals, they remain unable to coordinate and legitimate their resistance to the old regime at the national level. Without the intellectuals and the vanguard there may be "mutinous" local armies, even bandit armies, and there may be a "rebellion," but there is no *revolution* at the national level that succeeds in making a major property transfer.

2.4   To which revolutions do these remarks on the role of intellectuals in revolution-making apply? Primarily to *successful* revolutions, for I am concerned to distinguish successful revolutions from failures. Successful revolutions are those in which (a) the old state apparatus was destroyed (especially its repressive apparatus) and replaced by a new one, and in which (b) a major property transfer occurred. The two are connected, for a major property transfer, expropriating a powerful old class, probably cannot be accomplished successfully without the prior destruction of the state apparatus which had protected that class. I am, moreover, not interested here in those revolutions in which the property transfer strengthened a bourgeois, middle class, or a moneyed class. In other words, my remarks are not meant to apply to *bourgeois* revolutions which place increased proportions of the means of production into *private* hands. Moreover, I am referring to revolutions where the property transfer takes the form of a collectivization of private property that increases the means of production at the disposal of the *state* apparatus. In the first, bourgeois revolutions, power passes from those controlling land to those investing stocks of money capital; in the second, collectivizing revolutions, power passes from those whose incomes derive from money investments or landed property to those with "human capital,"[20] i.e., with relatively advanced education.[21]

# Thesis Three: New Class, Visible and Invisible

*3.1*  In revolutionary politics aiming at a mass mobilization, a visibly leading role for members of the new class is dissonant with the movement's populistic, egalitarian or communal emphases. There is pressure, then, to disguise, gloss, ignore, deny, or distort the New Class's importance in movements of a revolutionary character. The New Class in revolutionary politics has been an invisible class. It is the special task of critical theory and critical theorists to block the repression of the New Class's revolutionary role, and help this surface to public visibility.

*3.2*  In advanced industrial societies the New Class is not only sometimes *politically* revolutionary, but also constantly revolutionizes the mode of production. In these economies, the New Class serves as a technical intelligentsia whose work is subordinate to the old moneyed class. The New Class is useful to the old for the technical services it performs and, also, to legitimate the society as modern and scientific. To some extent, then, the New Class can have an open, public presence and its role can be acknowledged in advanced industrial economies. Here, it need not be invisible.

3.3   The New Class accepts its subordinate role in advanced economies, largely because (and *insofar* as) this is consistent with its material and ideal interests. In short, with its privileged style of life *and* its ability to pursue its own technical interests.

3.4   In the West, the New Class of intellectuals and intelligentsia pursues its class interests, both material and ideal, in various ways, including negotiation and resistance. Like other subordinated classes, the New Class does not get all that it wants or believes to be its due; it resists its subordination, and attempts to better its position.

3.5   The New Class's capacity to pursue its own aggrandizement and overcome the resistance of the old (moneyed) class, is, however, considerably greater than other subordinated classes. Because of its technical knowledge of the forces of production and means of administration, the New Class already has considerable *de facto* control over the mode of production and hence considerable leverage with which to pursue its interests. The new and old classes pursue a *contest* for control over the machinery of production and administration. This is partly a contest between the class which has *legal ownership* of the mode of production and the class whose technical knowledge increasingly gives it effective *possession* of the mode of production.

3.6   There is extensive and replicated evidence that managers, men having great power without commensurate property, are slowly placing the old moneyed class on the historical shelf. Yet studies of the growing split between ownership and management are not as unambiguous as it is sometimes held. The excellent critical review of the evidence, by Maurice Zeitlin, states that he "does not provide any answers to this question." His final conclusion is essentially methodological and "negative": ". . . the absence of control of proprietary interests in the largest corporations is by no means an 'unquestionable,' 'incontrovertible,' 'singular,' or 'critical' social 'fact.' "[22]
Zeitlin, however, acknowledges that the accepted view among the experts is that ownership has indeed become passive and control has entered the hands of professional management; that nonowning man-

agers are displacing moneyed capitalists. Zeitlin's is essentially a rear-guard action. He correctly notes that the careful qualifications that Berle and Means gave of their statistical analysis have often been lost to view and that others have too easily concluded that their research unqualifiedly documents management control. Zeitlin concludes that "they had information which permitted them to classify as definitely under management control only 22% of the 200 largest corporations."

Yet one wonders why Zeitlin says "only." Especially since this referred to the extent of management control almost *half a century ago*, in 1929. How much management control of large corporations is a "lot" and how much is "little"? Better still: the important question about management control is *not* how much there is *at any one time, but the secular trend*. Is management control becoming more or less, growing or declining, over the long duration? It would be immensely significant, even if management were in control of only a minority of the large corporations at any one time, if this was *continually increasing*.

For myself, then, the question is *not* the one Zeitlin asks, namely, whether the "largest corporations are [now] virtually all under management control." My own interests are in what is *becoming*.

Zeitlin cites a study by Philip Burch covering the period 1950–1971 which concludes that 58% of the 50 largest industrial corporations are "probably" under management control and that 40% of the largest 300 were "probably" under management control. To characterize management control as "probable" of course does not diminish the force of these findings any more than Burch's parallel remark that 45% of the largest 300 industrial corporations were "probably" under family control diminishes the significance of private ownership. The two "probablies" cancel one another—probably. Nor is it important that family control exceeds management control by 5% in the largest 300 industrial companies. Once again, the important consideration is the trend line: is management control declining or increasing; is family control? While rigorous historical evidence is difficult to come by, the long range trend seems clear. Even from the cross-sectional data that Zeitlin himself cites, it is clear that management control is already massive.

No one seems to believe that because the Soviet Constitution holds that the means of production in the USSR are publicly owned by the Soviet citizenry that this tells us very much about who actually controls Soviet industry and who profits from it. In considering the Soviet Union, it is widely recognized that legal ownership is largely of little importance for the everyday life of workers. Yet, in examining the late capitalist United States, considerable energy is expended in determining the role of ownership. The "left" tells us that here ownership still means a great deal, although it increasingly doubts that it means much when considering Soviet industry.

In answering Peter Drucker's contention that workers were gradu- ally buying up the means of production, through investment of their pension funds, and that there is emerging a kind of "pension-fund" socialism, the left replies, and with considerable reason, "that, though the pension funds may be *owned* by the unions, they are managed by the big banks and investment institutions. When a union turns its pension fund over to a bank, and that bank in turn invests the money in stock, it is the bank, not the union, that controls the stock votes." [23] For some, then, when considering investments made by *unions*, the important thing is that they do not control them even if they own them; but, when considering investments by *capitalists*, the important thing is that they own them. Doubtless, *both* are important; but most important of all is the secular trend. Is management control without property increasing over time? That is the question. It would be consistent with our argument to suggest that the *secular trend* favors professional management.

Just as we ought not to ask how much influence the New Class now has but how its influence in the economy is growing, so, too, we should always ask, influence in *which* institutional sector, over *which* kinds of decisions? Are, for example, New Class types increasing in the world's *military*, as armed force hardware becomes increasingly technical and scientized? And are these new generals merely pliable "servants of power"? Again, and to follow up on Christopher Lasch's suggestions, [24] clearly the New Class among the "helping" professions is increasing its influence over the welfare, the education, the life styles, the mental and physical health of families. Similarly, why have commentators such as Daniel Moynihan complained about the hostility of the press and other media to government, if the old class still retained its former hold on them? And how can universities still be under the same sway of the old class as the state's role in education grows?

Viewed historically, there is a "progressively greater arrogation of decisional competence by the intelligentsia in increasingly diverse areas. While the New Class starts out by critiquing traditional norma- tive systems (à la Voltaire and Diderot) in the name of reason and in the service of the potential political hegemony of the bourgeoisie, they conclude by arrogating to themselves not only administrative decisional competence but, finally, even the role of judges and regulators of the normative structures of contemporary societies. Jurgen Habermas' revival of German Idealism is making essentially the latter claim." [25]

Is the New Class now the ruling class? Certainly not. Will the New Class someday become the ruling class? Conceivably. If they are on their way to rule, what is taking them so long about it? But why assume it *is* taking them "long"?

How long did it take the *old* class to come into power? It had been emerging with urbanization and the waning of the "spiritual" power since perhaps the fourteenth century; in other words, for about four centuries before the revolution of 1789. The New Class has scarcely reached its maturity; indeed, it has only recently begun to reproduce itself. As Table I indicates, it has only been from about 1900 to 1930 that the New Class went through its "take-off" period in the United States.

# TABLE I

## The "Take-Off" Period of the New Class in the USA

Population of the New Class (in thousands,
except for total population in millions)

|  | 1870 | 1880 | 1900 | 1910 | 1920 | 1930 |
|---|---|---|---|---|---|---|
| Engineers | 5.6 | 7 | 38 | 77 | 134 | 217 |
| Managers (Manufg.) | 57 | — | — | 126 | 250 | 313 |
| Social, recreation, religious—not clergy | — | — | — | 19 | 46 | 71 |
| College faculty | 5.6 | 11.6 | 24 | — | 49 | 82 |
| Accountants, auditors | — | — | 23 | 39 | 118 | 192 |
| Gov't. officials, administrators, inspectors | — | — | 58 | 72 | 100 | 124 |
| Editors, reporters | — | — | 32 | — | 41 | 61 |
| Total population | 39.9 | 50.3 | 76.1 | 92.4 | 106.5 | 123.1 |

From: Barbara and John Ehrenreich, "The Professional Managerial Class," *Radical America* (March–April 1977), p. 19.

# Thesis Four: Arenas of Contest

*4.1* The emergence of intellectuals and intelligentsia onto the national political scene in American life does not seem significant until Woodrow Wilson's administration and until the involvement of intellectuals in the Socialist and Progressive Movements that preceded it.[26] Following the "muckraking" movement and World War I there is evidence of a growing alienation of American intellectuals. This is intensified by the Great Depression of the Thirties and by the anti-War and anti-Fascist movements. McCarthyism also did much to alienate and politicize American intellectuals. In time, they tended to develop their own favorite candidates in national elections, including Adlai Stevenson, Eugene McCarthy, Hubert Humphrey, and George McGovern. If the New Class in the United States has not yet been successful in electing its candidates, it has at least evidenced power in unseating one President, Lyndon Johnson. It was not the trade unions, the press, or businessmen, observed John Galbraith, who forced Johnson's retirement, but the universities who led the opposition to the war in Vietnam.

Intellectuals (as distinct from intelligentsia) have a clear party preference in the United States. They are united in their distaste for the Republican Party and by their preference for the Democrats. Charles Kadushin and his associates have observed that this is particularly true of opinion leaders among them: ". . . almost all elite intellectuals vote Democrat."[27]

*4.2* There are, at the level of public controversy, different *arenas* in the contest between the new and old classes: (1) Academic freedom has been a recurring issue in which academicians and old class members of the University's Board of Trustees[28] have contested with one another. (2) The protection of "consumer" rights has, since the days of "muckraking," been an issue that the New Class has used to "rake" the old class. (3) Unexpectedly enough, even the development of Scientific Management was in part a critique of waste within the business system and of business' reluctance to employ the most efficient methods. (4) The drive to use "brain trusts" and experts in public policy development served to limit the old class's influence on government, as well as that of the political machines with which it worked. (5) The development of an "independent" Civil Service has had much the same implication. (6) Reform movements seeking "honesty in government" are a perennial device of the New Class against the old which has long been used to paying for the political favors it wished. (7) The new international ecology movement, with its critique of wasted raw materials and energy supplies and of the pollution of the environment, is only the most recent strategy in the New Class's guerila warfare against the old class.[29] (8) Some important part of Women's Liberation is not only an expression of resistance to the oppression of women-in-general but a demand by educated, middle class women for full membership rights in the New Class.

4.3   The influence of the New Class spreads to the *investment of capital* as well as to the management of production. The old investing class is slowly transformed into a privileged but functionless status group, into a "nobility" without a function in production and administration. Step by step, the New Class of intellectuals transforms the old class into a rentier class, into pensioners living off their profits, rents, and interest, or into reorganizing their class character by taking over that of the New Class.

4.4   Short of going to the barricades, the New Class may harass the old, sabotage it, critique it, expose and muckrake it, express moral, technical, and cultural superiority to it, and hold it up to contempt and ridicule. The New Class, however, does not seek struggle for its own sake. No class does. It is concerned simply about securing its own material and ideal interests with minimum effort. Class struggle is only one device in a larger repertoire with which the New Class pursues its interests. No class goes to war without first seeing what it can secure through negotiation or threat.

4.5   One basic class strategy of the New Class is to cultivate an alliance with a mass working class, proletariat or peasantry, to sharpen the conflict between that mass and the old class, and to direct that alliance against the old class and its hegemonic position in the old social order.

4.6   A "welfare" state and a "socialist" state are both political strategies of the New Class. An essential difference is that in a socialist state, the hegemony of the New Class is fuller, its control over the working class is greater. In the welfare state (a) the new and the old class mutually limit one another and (b) share control over the working class, although (c) the New Class may at times ally itself with the working class to improve its own position against the old class.

# Thesis Five: The New Class as a Cultural Bourgeoisie

5.1   The New Class and the old class are at first undifferentiated; the New Class commonly originates in classes with property advantages, that is, in the old class, or is sponsored by them. The New Class of intellectuals and intelligentsia are the relatively more *educated* counterpart—often the brothers, sisters, or children—of the old moneyed class. Thus the New Class contest sometimes has the character of *a civil war within the upper classes*. It is the differentiation of the old class into contentious factions. To understand the New Class contest it is vital to understand how the *privileged* and advantaged, not simply the suffering, come to be alienated from the very system that privileges them.

5.2   The "non-negotiable" objectives of the old moneyed class are to reproduce their capital, at a minimum, but, preferably, to make it accumulate and to appropriate profit: M-C-M', as Marx said. This is done within a structure in which all of them must compete with one another. This unrelenting competition exerts pressure to rationalize their productive and administrative efforts and unceasingly to heighten efficiency. (Marx called it, "revolutionizing" production.) But this rationalization is dependent increasingly on the efforts of the New Class intelligentsia and its expert skills. It is inherent in its structural situation, then, that the old class must bring the New Class into existence.

5.3   Much of the New Class is at first trained under the direct control of the old class' firms or enterprises. Soon, however, the old class is separated from the reproduction of the New Class by the emergence and development of a public system of education whose costs are "socialized." [30]

5.4 The more that the New Class's reproduction derives from specialized systems of public education, the more the New Class develops an ideology that stresses its *autonomy*, its separation from and presumable independence of "business" or political interests. This autonomy is said to be grounded in the specialized knowledge or cultural capital transmitted by the educational system, along with an emphasis on the obligation of educated persons to attend to the welfare of the collectivity. In other words, the *ideology* of "professionalism" emerges. [31]

5.5 Professionalism is one of the public *ideologies* of the New Class, and is the genteel subversion of the old class by the new. Professionalism is a phase in the historical development of the "collective consciousness" of the New Class. While not overtly a critique of the old class, professionalism is a tacit claim by the New Class to *technical and moral superiority* over the old class, implying that the latter lack technical credentials and are guided by motives of commercial venality. Professionalism silently installs the New Class as the paradigm of virtuous and legitimate authority, performing with technical skill and with dedicated concern for the society-at-large. Professionalism makes a focal claim for the legitimacy of the New Class which tacitly de-authorizes the old class.

On the one side, this is a bid for prestige *within* the established society; on the other, it tacitly presents the New Class as an *alternative* to the old. In asserting its own claims to authority, professionalism in effect *devalues the authority of the old class.*

5.6 The special privileges and powers of the New Class are grounded in their *individual* control of special cultures, languages, techniques, and of the skills resulting from these. The New Class is a cultural bourgeoisie who appropriates privately the advantages of an historically and collectively produced cultural capital. Let us be clear, then: the New Class is not just *like* the old class; its special culture is not just *like* capital. No metaphor is intended. The special culture of the New Class *is* a stock of capital that generates a stream of income (some of) which it appropriates privately.

5.7 The fundamental objectives of the New Class are: to increase its own share of the national product; to produce and reproduce the special social conditions enabling them to appropriate privately larger shares of the incomes produced by the special cultures they possess; to control their work and their work settings; and to increase their political power partly in order to achieve the foregoing. The struggle of the New Class is, therefore, to *institutionalize a wage system*, i.e., a social system with a distinct principle of distributive justice: "from each according to his ability, to each according to his work," which is also the norm of "socialism." Correspondingly, the New Class may oppose other social systems and their different systems of privilege, for example, systems that allocate privileges and incomes on the basis of controlling stocks of money (i.e., old capital). The New Class, then, is prepared to be egalitarian so far as the privileges of the *old* class are concerned. That is, under certain conditions it is prepared to remove or restrict the special incomes of the old class: profits, rents, interest. The New Class is anti-egalitarian, however, in that it seeks special guild advantages—political powers and incomes—on the basis of its possession of cultural capital.

5.8    The New Class *is* a *new* class: it is neither identical to the old working class nor to the old moneyed class; while sharing elements of both, it also has characteristics possessed by neither. Like the working class, the New Class earns its living through its labor in a wage system; but unlike the old working class, it is basically committed to controlling the content of its work and its work environment, rather than surrendering these in favor of getting the best wage bargain it can negotiate. The New Class's consciousness is thus not "economistic." It is committed to producing worthy objects and services and to the development of the skills requisite for these. It is, therefore, not simply a proletariat alienated from work which is experienced—in Marx's image—as a process in which the dead products of past human labor dominate its own living labor in the present. Aspiring to produce worthy objects and services, the New Class must also be concerned to control its work environment. The New Class thus embodies any future hope of working class self-management and prefigures the release from alienated labor. That, on the one side.

But if the New Class is committed to its work and skills and the production of quality objects, it is not, however, committed to these without an interest in their accompanying incomes. The New Class seeks both incomes *and* quality objects, but does not aim at the latter simply to procure the former. The New Class is not selflessly dedicated to its arts, yet these are not merely instrumental to its incomes.

The New Class's occupational culture is neither the caricature of the devoted professional selflessly sacrificing himself in the service of his clients, nor is it the stereotype of the venal elite that prostitutes its skills for gain.

Just as the New Class is not the proletariat of the past, neither is it the old bourgeoisie. It is, rather, a new *cultural* bourgeoisie whose capital is not its money but its control over valuable cultures. A systematic comparison of the New Class and the old class would ultimately require analysis of different forms of capital, of stocks of culture versus stocks of money. Both are forms of capital as each is a source of an ongoing stream of income. What is needed for the systematic analysis of the old and new class is a *general theory of capital* in which moneyed capital is seen as part of the whole, as a special case of capital. Conversely, what is required for the understanding of culture as capital is nothing less than a political economy of culture.[32] Although not possible here, some tentative indications are developed below.

*5.9 Notes on Capital and Cultural Capital;*   Capital—to define it succinctly but generally—is: any produced object used to make saleable utilities, thus providing its possessor with *incomes*, or claims to incomes defined as legitimate because of their imputed contribution to economic productivity; these claims to income are enforced normally by withholding, or threatening to withhold, the capital-object. Thus while capital (of *any* kind) does not necessarily increase productivity, it is culturally *defined* as contributing to productivity, making possible the typical way that capital enforces its claims to incomes: i.e., by modifying others' access to the capital-object, or threatening to do so.

*5.10*   Just as it is not true that education necessarily increases productivity, neither can it be assumed that *any other* form of capital necessarily increases productivity,[33] although, like education, it *may* do so. A demystified theory of human capital (or education *qua* capital) must be part of a more general critique of capital that recognizes that the first concern of capital is with its *incomes*, not with its productivity, with its own partisan perquisites rather than its contribution to society. This is much of what Thorstein Veblen intended with his distinction between "business" and "industry," whose differing interests could, he noted, conflict. Capital, i.e., *any* form of capital, will, if it can, increase its income even where this does not increase productivity. Capital's contribution to productivity occurs primarily when its own incomes are *necessarily* linked to increased productivity.

5.11    A basic strategy of any form of capital, traditional or human, is to dissociate its incomes from its performances, so that its incomes will continue even when its performances fail. A second basic strategy, of course, is to conceal such failures. Capital, then, seeks "something for nothing"—as Veblen put it. The link between capital's incomes and its performances was forged historically by competition which *constrained* capital to enhance productivity lest it be destroyed by others who did so. But competition, of course, could be limited by monopolies, cartels and other arrangements among capital owners, thus severing the connection between income and productivity. Much the same control over competition occurs among owners of human capital, through professional and other types of organizations, and with a resulting dissociation between their incomes and their productivity. Another basic tactic, allowing discrepancies between incomes and performances, is for the performing group to seek complete authority to judge its own performances, thus allowing it to conceal its failures, and any resulting disparity between its performances and its incomes.

5.12    The use of any form of capital may occur because it facilitates claims on incomes or where it enables controls to be established over the economic process. Increased uses of conventional capital are not always demonstrably associated with increases in productivity, but may be employed because they reduce dependence on other groups involved in the economic process, placing the latter and its surplus under the *control* of those possessing capital. Capital may not merely *increase* production but may also permit it to be *controlled*. [34]

5.13    Capital, then, is a produced object whose public goal is increased economic productivity but whose latent function is to increase the incomes and social control of those possessing it. In this perspective it is plain that education is as much capital as are a factory's buildings or machines.

5.14    To expand upon the general concept of capital formulated above:
    (1) Capital is a *produced* object rather than a "natural" raw material or even an inborn talent and is as such a product of both human *labor and culture.*

(2) It is also a product not employed for its consummatory satisfactions, but in order to produce *other* utilities and wealth. The object of capital is not consumption but instrumental mastery. It is thus "goods producing goods."

(3) There is no way to determine whether something is an item of "consumption" or is "capital" without knowing the aims and *intentions* of those using it. Nothing is capital unless used with the *intention* of producing something economically valuable; nothing is *inherently* capital. Correspondingly, *any* produced object used with the intention of augmenting utilities or wealth whether hardware or skills, may be capital—if it conforms with the additional stipulations outlined below.

(4) Anything is capital when it serves as the basis of enforceable claims to the private appropriation of incomes legitimated for their contribution to the production of economic valuables or wealth Capital differs, then, from fraud, force, violence, or domination that are used to extort wealth as ransom, loot, booty, or tribute. Capital is neither theft nor extortion but acknowledges the norm of *reciprocity*, claiming that it is *entitled* to what it gets because of what it has contributed.

(5) The enforceable claims to the private appropriation of incomes entailed by capital are typically sanctioned by factors *intrinsic* to the capital-object itself. The threat of withholding it, or the actual withholding of it, will typically suffice to enforce claims upon incomes because it is (or is defined as) "necessary" for the production of economic utilities. Capital, then, premises a structural differentiation between economic and political-military subsystems and their different sanctioning systems, the latter being used by capital only as a last resort, or in the event of defaults in promised returns for the use of capital-objects.

(6) Capital has access to incomes not because it necessarily increases productivity or wealth, but simply because its income claims are socially enforceable and culturally recognized. The education of the New Class is part of its capital. It is not capital because it necessarily increases productivity, but simply because it provides incomes, because these incomes are enforceable, *and* because they are legitimated intrinsically, depending on the continued availability or withholding of their services and activities.

5.15 While capital of any kind *need not* increase productivity, and while its claims to incomes may be enforceable even where it does not increase productivity, there is a tendency for this situation to become a form of "domination," where incomes are extracted by the threat or use of force or violence. For without an increase in productivity, an improvement in anyone's income takes place through a zero-sum game in which one group's loss is another's gain and vice versa. Where productivity is increasing, however, the income of any group may be maintained or even increased without loss to another. Where capital yields increases in productivity, then, the threat to withhold or withdraw it will more readily suffice to enforce its claims upon incomes and incomes will here be protected by intrinsic enforcers.

5.16   The availability of political and military sanctions for extracting incomes thus limits the development of capital, for each may be used as a substitute for the other. Correspondingly, the inhibition of political and military sanctions in the economic process is conducive to the development and use of capital with its *intrinsically* enforceable claim on income. Elimination of "private enterprise" threatens the efficient use and development of capital, particularly of traditional bourgeois capital. At the same time, the elimination of traditional bourgeois capital makes the economic process increasingly dependent on the kinds of cultural capital and technological skills of the New Class who become the principal societal locus of capital development and of intrinsically enforceable claims to income.

As the New Class's ability to enforce its income claims grows, it must either be coopted into the ruling class or it must be subjected to the repressive control of a burgeoning bureaucracy. Being intrinsically enforceable, the New Class's claims on incomes become the principal limit on the claims of military and political authorities, i.e., the state apparatus, and the New Class inherits the critique of the state once invested in the old propertied middle class. Their critique of the state now, however, takes the mystified form of asserting the dominance and autonomy of impersonal technology.

5.17   The new ideology holds that productivity depends primarily on science and technology and that the society's problems are solvable on a technological basis, and with the use of educationally acquired technical competence. While this ideology de-politicizes the public realm, and, in part, *because* it does this, it cannot be understood simply as legitimating the *status quo*, for the ideology of the autonomous technological process delegitimates all other social classes than the New Class. The use of science and technology as a legitimating ideology serves the New Class, lauding the functions it performs, the skills it possesses, the educational credentials it owns, and thereby strengthens the New Class's claims on incomes *within the status quo* in which it finds itself. Presenting technology as an impersonal and autonomous societal resource, the New Class conceals itself and its own role in the process, as well as the way in which it is pursuing a renegotiation of incomes advantageous to itself.

5.18 The theory of culture as capital begins, it seems, with none other than the putative father of sociology, Auguste Comte himself, the secretary and "ungrateful" disciple of the great utopian socialist Henri Saint-Simon. In his *System of Social Polity*,[35] second chapter, Comte commented on the origins of capital in labor, in the human ability to produce more than it can consume—i.e., a surplus—and in the durability of some of this, thus permitting its cumulation over generations and its transmission through time. But this is exactly what is entailed by the anthropological concept of "culture." Comte was at that early juncture between political economy and sociology, where culture and capital mixed and were interchangeable, and where one might say that either capital *or* culture was "the basis of social development." The emerging concepts of "culture" and "capital" were Siamese twins, joined at the back: culture was capital generalized and capital was culture privatized.

In effect, it was the transformation of culture into *property*, whose incomes could be appropriated or bequeathed *privately*, that the classical political economists had termed "capital." Capital was the private appropriation of culture, the private enclosure of the cultural commons.

5.19 If any part of culture is to be "capital" there must be private appropriation of the goods it produces, when this is protected by custom and the state. Culture becomes capital when it is "capitalized," which means when incomes are set aside for those possessing culture or certain forms of it, while denying these incomes to those lacking it. Capital then is inherently an advantage; those having it are secured gratifications denied to those lacking it. The provision of special incomes for those possessing any culturally acquired skill through wages, royalties, patents, copyrights, or credentialling is the capitalization of the skill.

*Credentialling* is the certification by someone or some group, taken to be a competent authority, that the individual in question possesses certain cultural skills. The preemption of certain offices, livings, or jobs—like the setting apart of incomes—for those properly credentialled, as in any bureaucratic, meritocratic, or civil service system, is the capitalization of these cultural skills. Culture is transmitted through education and socialization. Generally, it is known that those with more formal education have life-time earnings in excess of those with less, although it appears that each increment of education produces declining increments of additional incomes.[36] This increased income reflects the capital value of increased education; i.e., increased income implies that the culture for which it is paid has been capitalized at a value in proportion to the amount of education it took to learn it.

5.20    Consider: a man starts a business with a certain capital sum and having built it up over the years decides to sell it. How much does it sell for? Its sale price is a function of its prospective *income*, not the original capital investment. The sale price is the income capitalized. Income then has a capital equivalence; capital is the discounted value of future income and differential incomes imply different capitalizations.

5.21    The capital value of anything is the discounted value of the size of the incomes it is expected to produce, the amount in ready money its incomes can be exchanged for. Since the economic value of incomes is expressible as a discounted capital sum, there is an interchangeability between income and capital.

Since capital value depends in part on the size of the incomes it produces, anything—including culture—that increases these incomes also increases its capital value, and conversely. The size of incomes yielded by culture, and hence the capital value, is a function of the supply of and demand for it, and of its prospective lifetime or perishability. The interests of the cultural bourgeoisie, then, dispose it to control the supply and limit the production of its culture, to oppose any group that restricts its control over its culture, and to remove legal or moral restriction on the uses for which its culture may be purchased. Underneath "professionalism," there is the political economy of culture.

5.22    Classical political economy, as the ideology of the rising bourgeoisie, tended to define capital in a limited way, as the kind of capital possessed by the bourgeoisie. Certainly the form of capital

controlled by the bourgeoisie was then, indeed, the "chief" part—
which is what *"capital"* originally means. Marxism accepted political
economy's dichotomy between moneyed property and labor, and
tended to reckon labor in units of simple manual labor, assigning a
cultural function primarily to the entrepreneur and management. But
"labor" is not simply energy expended, but energy expended in conformity to some cultural requirement or standard, a norm. Thus labor
need not directly involve persons at all. All it requires is an expendi-
ture of energy controlled by a feedback system that monitors its conformity with a norm. Labor creates value, as does any energy input,
only when conforming to a cultural norm. Since the amount of energy
available and the form to which it submits is a function of culture, the
value of labor is a function of the cultural investment.

5.23 Classical political economy and radicalized political economy—
i.e., Marxism—were both grounded in an historical experience with a
labor force that, on the average, had a low degree of skill. Overgen-
eralizing from this limited historical experience, they could tacitly
treat cultural capital as if it were nil. But the great growth in cultural
capital since that time calls for a new general theory of capital, for a
political economy of culture, and for a theory of a New Class as cul-
ture-privileged, and where private ownership of moneyed capital is
seen as only a special case of "capitalism." An investment in education is not simply a consumable. Something is left over, which produces a subsequent flow of income. It is *cultural capital*, the
economic basis of the New Class.

5.24 The possession of cultural capital both unites and separates the
New Class from the working class. The New Class's possession of cultural capital is not unique, for all classes possess it in some degree.
Since all have some cultural capital, how, then, does the New Class
differ from others? In two ways: first, *quantitatively* [37]—it possesses a
relatively great stock of it, and a relatively larger part of its income
derives from it. Second, *qualitatively*—its culture is a special one, in
some part. In this connection, the New Class of intellectuals and intelligentsia is distinguished by the fact it is also a *speech* community.
They speak a special linguistic variant, an elaborated linguistic
variant. Their speech variant is characterized by an orientation to a
qualitatively special culture of speech: to the culture of careful and
critical discourse (CCD).

# Thesis Six: The New Class as a Speech Community

6.1   The culture of critical discourse (CCD)[38] is an historically evolved set of rules, a grammar of discourse, which (1) is concerned to *justify* its assertions, but (2) whose *mode* of justification does not proceed by invoking authorities, and (3) prefers to elicit the *voluntary* consent of those addressed solely on the basis of arguments adduced. CCD is centered on a specific speech act: justification. It is a culture of discourse in which there is nothing that speakers will on principle permanently refuse to discuss or make problematic; indeed, they are even willing to talk about the value of talk itself and its possible inferiority to silence or to practice. This grammar is the deep structure of the common ideology shared by the New Class. *The shared ideology of the intellectuals and intelligentsia is thus an ideology about discourse.* Apart from and underlying the various technical languages (or sociolects) spoken by specialized professions, intellectuals and intelligentsia are commonly committed to a culture of critical discourse (CCD). CCD is the latent but mobilizable infrastructure of modern "technical" languages.

6.2   The culture of critical discourse is characterized by speech that is *relatively* more *situation-free*, more context or field "independent." This speech culture thus values expressly legislated meanings and devalues tacit, context-limited meanings. Its ideal is: "one word, one meaning," for everyone and forever.

The New Class's special speech variant also stresses the importance of particular modes of *justification*, using especially explicit and articulate rules, rather than diffuse precedents or tacit features of the speech context. The culture of critical speech requires that the validity of claims be justified without reference to the speaker's *societal position or authority*. Here, good speech is speech that can make its own principles *explicit* and is oriented to conforming with them, rather than stressing context-sensitivity and context-variability. Good speech here thus has *theoreticity*.[39]

Being pattern-and-principle-oriented, CCD implies that that which is said may *not* be correct, and may be *wrong*. It recognizes that "What Is" may be mistaken or inadequate and is therefore open to alternatives. CCD is also relatively more *reflexive*, self-monitoring, capable of more meta-communication, that is, of talk about talk; it is able to make its own speech problematic, and to edit it with respect to its lexical and grammatical features, as well as making problematic the validity of its assertions. CCD thus requires considerable "expressive discipline," not to speak of "instinctual renunciation."

6.3    Most importantly, the culture of critical speech forbids reliance upon the speaker's person, authority, or status in society to justify his claims. As a result, CCD de-authorizes all speech grounded in traditional societal authority, while it authorizes itself, the elaborated speech variant of the culture of critical discourse, as the standard of *all* "serious" speech. From now on, persons and their social positions must not be visible in their speech. Speech becomes impersonal. Speakers hide behind their speech. Speech seems to be disembodied, de-contextualized and self-grounded. (This is especially so for the speech of intellectuals and somewhat less so for technical intelligentsia who may not invoke CCD except when their paradigms break down.) The New Class becomes the guild masters of an invisible pedagogy.

6.4    The culture of critical discourse is the common ideology shared by the New Class, although technical intelligentsia sometimes keep it in latency. The skills and the social conditions required to reproduce it are among the common *interests* of the New Class. Correspondingly, it is in the common interest of the New Class to prevent or oppose all censorship of its speech variety and to install it as the standard of good speech. *The New Class thus has both a common ideology in CCD and common interests in its cultural capital.*

6.5 *Query:*    Is the New Class actually "unified" by its common rules of discourse? Are not intellectuals perpetual malcontents, eternally outside of any class? Are not technical intelligentsia (because they operate *within* "paradigms") necessarily conservative? Let us take the last question first.

*Technical intelligentsia* center their work on the detailed development of the paradigm dominant in their technical specialty. Where that specialty is mature, there may only be one paradigm, but often there are more. Where there are several, the technical intelligentsia face this alternative: either they abandon discussion with one another, alleging a total "incommensurability of paradigms," or they must reactivate the latent common culture of critical discourse underlying their technical language. Any problem with a paradigm, is characteristically resolved then by recourse to CCD. People must give reasons; they cannot rely upon their position in society or in their science to justify technical decisions. (In this way, they are substantially different from *bureaucrats*, even when pursuing "normal science.") And even when operating within a single paradigm, an accumulation of anomolous findings requires them to revise or abandon the paradigm, which they are able to do only by reverting once again to the culture of critical discourse.

*In short, CCD is a common bond between humanistic intellectuals and technical intelligentsia*, as well as among different technical intelligentsia themselves. As a language, CCD unifies in much the same way as ordinary languages, say French or German. Just as French and German are boundary-establishing, unifying elements, making it easier for members of the nation to communicate with one another, but making it harder for them to do so with people who do not speak their language, so, too, does CCD unify those who use it and establish distance between themselves and those who do not.

This does not mean, of course, that there are no significant differences between those who speak German, or CCD; it does not mean that those who speak German, or CCD, might not be seriously divided or be hostile to one another in some ways. Still, despite those divisions, there is a special solidarity brought by the sharing of a language.

In speaking of the New Class as a "class," the question commonly arises as to how unitary, cohesive, or solidary they are or can be, how homogeneous in their interests, culture, and policies, and whether these are or can be opposed to the old moneyed class. That members of the New Class *can* pursue a politics opposed to the old moneyed class seems obvious enough from their record, as discussed later in Thesis Ten on Revolutionary Intellectuals and, indeed, as indicated by their role as leading members of various terrorist groups. Clearly, there have also been important historical occasions when the New Class was widely united as, for example, during the anti-fascist movement of the 1930s and, more recently, in their opposition to the United States' war on Vietnam. What has been, can be. These cases of wide social solidarity among intellectuals and intelligentsia are deserving of closer historical study. The members of the New Class, whether intellectuals or intelligentsia, are also likely to have greater ease of social interaction with one another, precisely because of their similar education, culture, and language codes, thus facilitating development of coteries, social circles, professional ties and political projects among themselves. In addition to having friendly, informal, or intimate ties with one another, they are also more likely to reside and vacation in the same neighborhoods and ecological areas, as well as intermarrying frequently with one another.

The denial that the New Class can ever act in a solidary political way because of its internal differentiation, reminds one of similar claims once made about women's or blacks' capacity to form politically effective status groups. From some points of view, women should not be able to form coherent political movements because some are poor and others well off, some are Black and others white, some heterosexual and some homosexual, etc. Yet the women's movement grows and abides. Indeed, the working class itself has also been said to be too internally divided into different craft, industrial, and wage groups, sharply segmented by education, sex, race and age, and prey to nationalism and chauvinism; yet this has not aborted the rise of powerful working class political parties, trade unions, and movements. Indeed, the "capitalist class" itself has all manner of internal differences and, as Marx said, each capitalist destroys many others.

For the most part, classes themselves do not enter into active political struggle; the active participants in political struggle are usually organizations, parties, associations, vanguards. Classes are cache areas in which these organizations mobilize, recruit, and conscript support and in whose name they legitimate their struggle. Classes as such are never united in struggle against others. Moreover, there is no reason to suppose that the New Class, at least in "the West," will "overthrow" capital in a manner modelled after, say, the Russian October Revolution. Here, the New Class's rise will more nearly be like that of the bourgeoisie than like revolutions made in the name of the working class. That is, it will have hundreds of years of development, will consolidate itself through a Reformation, and have the time thoroughly to establish its own characteristic modes of production before they cap their rise with all the trappings of political authority.

*6.6 On Edward Shils:* Two theorists who are particularly useful in discerning the specific nature of the New Class's ideology are Basil

Bernstein, whose importance for our work has already been noted,[40] and Edward Shils,[41] who has formulated a more diffuse diagnosis of intellectuals' cultural characteristics. I will discuss Noam Chomsky also because, in some ways, his analysis of modern intellectuals sharply denies the "adversary" character that Shils imputes to them.

Shils has been exceptionally emphatic in stressing the *alienative* disposition of intellectuals which he derives from their special culture. He sees their culture as differing from others—the "laity" he calls them—for they are not limited to the at-hand immediacies of the everyday life. Intellectuals are more concerned than the "laity" with the more remote, with ultimate values, being disposed to go beyond direct, first-hand experience with the concrete and to live in a "wider universe." They are also more rule, value, pattern-oriented, or have more theoreticity than others who are more person-oriented, more situationally sensitive, and more responsive to differences in contexts.

Intellectuals, for Shils, are also more committed to the cultivation of alternatives, to possibilities and not only to realities: to what *might* be and not only to what *is*. Through the "elaboration" of tradition, says Shils, by systematization, thematization, explication, rationalization, and formalization, alternative possibilities are envisaged.

Shils derives the alienative potential of intellectuals from their special orientation to culture, as I, in *part*, derive it from their culture of critical discourse:

> The process of elaborating and developing further the potentialities inherent in a "system" of cultural values entails also the possibility of "rejection" of the inherited set of values. . . . In all societies, even in those in which intellectuals are notable for their conservatism, the diverse paths of creativity, as well as the inevitable tendency toward negativism, impel a partial rejection of the prevailing system of cultural values.[42]

Shils's discussion of the alienative disposition of intellectuals clearly entails a *critique* of intellectuals (rather than simply an appreciation) of their "enlightenment." This critique has a special focus: it limits itself primarily to intellectuals' disruption of social solidarity, to their break with *established tradition*, and to their opposition to *constituted authority*. What Shils does *not* consider is how the negativity of intellectuals embodies a disguised set of claims advancing their own candidacy as a new elite. Shils does not consider this as a contest of two elites, but simply as the nihilistic negativism of intellectuals that can end in anarchism and in the overthrow of all hierarchy. Shils thereby misses the possibility that the "negativity" of intellectuals is only the opening move in the replacement of the old by a new class, and of an old tradition and hierarchy by new ones.

Shils's critique of intellectuals is made from the standpoint of the old class and, indeed, of strata even more archaic than the old class. He speaks in the name of the "sacred" and of "tradition." When Shils says the "tradition of distrust of secular and ecclesiastical authority—and in fact of tradition as such—has become the chief secondary tradition of the intellectuals," he does not see intellectuals as a New Class but as priests *manquées*, as tutors of the New Princes, who should keep their place.

Shils's diagnosis of the *cultural* formation of intellectuals is useful, at least for *Western* intellectuals. This formation, he holds, involves four elements: scientism, romanticism, revolutionism, and populism, each of which has its own specific alienative potential. *Populism*, believing in the worth of ordinary persons and in the value of their simplicity and wisdom, may dispose intellectuals to praise the folk as truer and wiser than the more artificial, alien-influenced members of their own society's elite. The *revolutionary* tradition, Shils holds, draws on an ancient tradition of millenarianism in which the everyday world is seen as so profoundly divergent from sacred values, indeed as so corrupt and evil, as not to be amenable to partial reforms but as requiring an urgently necessary and imminent radical transformation. *Romanticism* revolts against rules and traditions seen as external, imposed, and alien, because they curb spontaneity, impulses, and creativity. Finally, *scientism* insists that neither external tradition nor internal impulse should be allowed to govern judgment which must, rather, rest on experience sifted by critical reflection. Thus all the specific traditions constituting the *cultural* formation of (Western) intellectuals spark rebellion against the tradition and authority in being.[43]

But there is a deeper structure that is shared by and underlies these several concrete traditions on which Shils focuses. This may be called "voluntarism" or perhaps better still, "self-groundedness." This encompasses and refers to the inner rather than the external, to the chosen rather than the imposed, to the indigenous rather than the alien, to the natural rather than the artificial. *It refers to that which is capable of self-movement and self-direction, rather than to that which is externally driven.* The deepest structure in the culture and ideology of intellectuals is their pride in their own *autonomy,* which they understand as based on their own reflection, and their ability to decide their course in the light of this reflection. Thus any authority that demands obedience or any tradition that demands conformity without reflection and decision is experienced as a tyrannical violation of self.

Autonomy, or self-groundedness, becomes one of the central ideals of modern intellectuals' notion of rationality. It is held that an argument must stand on its own legs, must be self-sufficient, that one must "consider the speech not the speaker," that it must encompass all that is necessary, providing a full presentation of the assumptions needed to produce and support the conclusion. This becomes a basic rule of the grammar of modern rationality, is most fully exhibited in the geometric proof with its comprehensive structure of axioms and theorems, and is at the bottom of what Heidegger called the "mathematical project." The basic ideology of discourse, as the ideology of intellectuals and intelligentsia, premises a sphere of autonomy in which speech and action are rule-oriented rather than causally controlled by external force; where conclusions are reflectively *selected* and constructed in the light of certain rules, rather than being imposed by force, tradition, impulse, or the imperative "laws" of science.

The emphasis on "autonomy," however, is not simply to be understood as a spiritual value important to intellectuals, or as desired because without it they are unable to work properly. Autonomy is not only a work requisite or an ethical aspiration but is, also, an expression of the social *interests* of the New Class as a distinct group. The stress on autonomy is the ideology of a stratum that is still subordinated to other groups whose limits it is striving to remove—partly consciously and in part unconsciously. This quest for autonomy expresses a *political* impulse toward that self-management of work characteristic of (at least) skilled and "professional" workers seeking to control "the terms, conditions and content of their work . . ." for *guild* reasons. [44]

More generally, Shils's perspective on the several cultural sources of modern intellectuals is one-sided in thinking of these as a *formation*. Focussing on them as elements that go into the making of modern intellectuals, he neglects the other side, namely, that they are also *made* by intellectuals under the impress of their own status group interests, that they are all aspects of intellectuals' ideology, and symptomatic of the emergence of the New Class.

Consider, for example, Shils's formulation of the significance of "scientism." Scientism is an inference made about the culture of intellectuals from an examination of more historically specific and concrete social movements in which intellectuals were at one time involved. Scientism, for example, is at best an inference from the meaning of early nineteenth century Positivism. This last, however, was surely not only an insistence that judgment should be decided by experience sifted by reason; indeed, this might even be the view of prudent businessmen. Positivism, rather, as it emerged in the work of Henri Saint-Simon and the Saint-Simonians, involved a view of the modern world as veritably based on science and technology, which they saw as being the universal interests of mankind. Science/technology was seen as crucial because it could overcome ancient scarcities and, through increasing productivity, bind the working class to society. Science would, also, *integrate* the new society, they expected, because it would provide certain (i. e., "positive") knowledge of what was true and hence a basis for common belief and social solidarity. The new industrial and positivist society was to be rescued from scarcity, integrated and legitimated by the new science and technology, and the new scientists/technocrats were to become the "priests" of this society.

Authority would then no longer rest upon inherited office or on force and violence—*or even property*—but on skill and science. In effect, Positivism was a premature bid by the emerging New Class to portray itself as the essential source of legitimacy and productivity in modern society. The new moneyed classes, however, only just beginning to wrest a place for themselves and fighting the old Regime's rearguard "restoration" action, were hardly about to accept this lordly view advanced by what was then a small and seedy sect. Any serious history of the New Class, then, must see historically specific Positivism (not vague "scientism") as a decisive moment in the early evolution of the New Class and of its emerging self-consciousness.

Shils's view of romanticism as a revolt against repressive and external rules is essentially correct, if simplified. One would add that romanticism also embodied a contempt of the "philistinism" of the new men of money, who valued only those things that made money. It was the moneyed philistines who now had the power to censor. [45] If the positivists held that the emerging moneyed class could not be legitimated without a grounding in the new sciences and technologies, the romantics insisted this would take more, their support for culture and the arts. At one level, then, both positivists and romantics agreed in their judgment of the new moneyed class, sneering at their deficiencies while offering to help overcome them. At the same time, the romantic emergence also implied a critique of the new science and technology—and their functionaries—in which the romantics saw a certain communality between their "materialism" and the philistinism of the moneyed class.

The new positivist engineers, scientists, physicians had a future in the new industrial order they first saw emerging in the early nineteenth century and thus their critique of it was ambivalent. Yet while they had a future in the new industrial society, it was only a subordinated place to which they might look forward. The positivists came to a critique of the moneyed class, or the bourgeoisie, because of this and because they feared that private industrial property, being privately inheritable, could fall into incompetent hands and waste a social resource. It was out of such motives that Saint-Simonian "utopian socialism" first emerged. The romantics, however, being artists, musicians, poets, novelists, had even less reason to compromise with the emerging bourgeoisie, for they had little prospect of a future in the new scientific order; they were at the mercy of market forces which, if liberating them from the personal domination of individual patrons, made their livelihoods precarious. The romantics thus began to "drop out" into the emerging bohemias, to wage a sniping guerilla warfare against the emerging new order, and began the building of a "counter-culture."

Marxism is dubiously understood, as Shils suggests, as the residue of an ancient millenarianism. Millenarianism was more likely to appeal to the *under*privileged and suffering rather than to the sons of the advantaged and privileged—the vanguard of the New Class—who created Marxism, and who were also highly secularized. Marxism is better understood as the fusion of both Romanticism and Positivism, and *in which a section of the alienated New Class is seeking a mass base in the proletariat*. Its message is that the world can be changed effectively only through the *scientific* understanding of society which it offers, not through a mere act of will. Like romanticism, Marxism's "labor theory of value" takes creativity as a central theme. Marxism, however, views the proletariat as the essential creative force in society, indeed as the only source of economic value and surplus value. Rather than retaining creativity as the charismatic gift of a small elite, Marxism makes this the exclusive possession of the deprived masses.

The linkages of Marxism to the New Class derive from both its positivist and romantic inheritances and, more than that, from its drive toward a socialism in which the expropriation of private property would not merely eliminate irrational limits on productivity, but would also remove the structural limit placed on the ambitions of the New Class under capitalism. With the overthrow of capitalism, there is no longer a bourgeoisie to which the New Class is subject. Marx viewed his work as superior to the "utopian socialism" of Saint-Simon and Fourier; but having worked before the massive appearance of the New Class he was not, however, the first of the scientific socialists but the last of the utopians.

6.7 *On Parsons and Habermas:* This is not the place for a history of the ideologies of the New Class and our remarks here are intended only as notes and suggestions for such a history. Central to such a history, of course, would be the ideologies of "professionalism," perhaps most especially among modern sociologists. Indeed, Talcott Parsons' vast *oeuvre* can best be understood as a complex ideology of the New Class, expressed by and through his flattering conception of *professionalism*. Parsons, in fact, defines modern society as characterized by professionalism rather than by its capitalist character. In this, Parsons emphasized the convergence between business and the professions, rather than the Veblenian divergence between business and industry. Parsons' focus was on the characteristics common to business and the professions; for example, there was presumably a common commitment to efficiency, with each accepting limited spheres of competence and authority, and each also being universalistic, governing by general and impersonal rules.[46] Parsons' conception of professionalism, then, largely serves to assimilate business to the professions, concealing business' overriding commitment to profit. By assimilating business to the collectivity-centeredness of the professions, Parsons provides a new legitimation for the old business class by intimating their impending moral revival.

Parsons' concept of the professions involves a shift from positivism, stressing their dedicated moral character rather than their grounding in science and codified knowledge. His view of the professions glosses their own self-seeking character as a status group with vested interests, thus ideologically romanticizing both the old and new class. Pursuing his usual effort to eliminate contradictions from social life, Parsons also ignores the tensions between the old and new classes and the ways in which the New Class ideology of professionalism tacitly *subverts* old class legitimacy by grounding itself in a moral collectivity orientation and in scientific knowledge and skills, lacking in the profit-pursuing egoism of the old class. Parsons' fundamental picture is that the new national elite of the United States will consist of a *revamped,* professionalized business class, allied and fused with New Class professionals. The rise of the New Class in the United States, in Parsons' view, will thus occur within the framework of a business society and through the moral uplift of the old class by the New Class. While still bound by respect and prudence toward the old class, which it conceives as aiming primarily at productivity for society rather than at incomes for itself, Parsons' sociology is characterized by an impulse to revitalize the legitimacy of the foundering old class by uniting it with the New Class and by professionalizing it.

Parsons vacillates between using the New Class as a prop to shore up the foundering old class, on the one side, and on the other, submitting the old class to a thoroughgoing reformation under the tutelage of the New Class. He seeks a compromise between it and the claims of the old class. Parsons' theory is thus an *uneasy* sociology of the New Class; it remains backward-looking, still convinced that the old class has something of a future, and mistakenly imagines that the old class's weaknesses are primarily weaknesses of legitimation. Parsons uses the New Class to solve the old class's "legitimation crisis."

From Positivism to Parsonianism, sociology (as a discipline) has been especially open to the claims and perspectives of the New Class. In its Positivistic beginnings sociology was *not* (as I plainly said in *The Coming Crisis of Western Sociology*) "the intellectual creation of the propertied middle class," but rather of a declassed nobility and "of a nascent technical intelligentsia" [47] which was at first literally disfranchised. While Parsons' own sociology initially emerged in a pre-welfare "state" situation, after the maturation of this state form, his own and other academic sociologies increasingly represent the claims of the New Class. Compared, for example, with academic economics, sociology clearly takes the standpoint of the New Class.

In its emphasis on the importance of a revitalized morality [48] as the basis for "critique" and practical discourse, Jürgen Habermas' critical theory is surprisingly convergent with the deep structure of Talcott Parsons' sociology. Unlike Parsons, however, Habermas has no sentimental attachments to the old moneyed class. He emphasizes, however, that the dangers of societal domination will not be removed simply by "socializing" the means of production. Habermas is critically alive to the New Class's elite proclivities, which he sees as undermining popular decision-making prerogatives.

Habermas most basically represents the internal struggle within the New Class, a struggle of an older humanistic elite against the newer technocratic elites, and especially focusses on the *anomie*-producing, de-moralizing effects of the technical intelligentsia's stress on instrumental efficiency. He seeks a new institutional framework— the "ideal speech situation"—within which not only technical means might be chosen, but which would also revitalize morality, and which would select the very goals to which technology would be applied. Habermas' aim, then, is to control the technical elite and facilitate popular participation in effective decision-making, by establishing the institutional requisites of a social system that could subordinate technicians to the requirements of a rational morality and practical reason, but which must also *subordinate them to the Guardians of this morality and reason.* Habermas' Critical Theory is a critique of the technical intelligentsia and the bureaucratic politics of "scientific" socialism, of both intelligentsia and bureaucracy, from the standpoint of an older humanistic elite. In his view, the old class is tacitly considered as historically obsolescent; the future is seen as divided between political and technical strata, both having strong elements of irrationality and elitism that need to be subjected to effective public controls and public goal-setting.

The Critical theorist is, in this view, the new Guardian of the moral grounding of social action, enabling the larger populace to play a more effective role in the practical discourse of public life, and subjecting the irrationalities and limits of technical and political elites to a transcending critique. Habermas' "apoliticism" represents the assumption that the transformations in consciousness he seeks can be achieved not by political revolution but by a cultural reformation. Such a critical theory, then, is the ideology of a morally concerned sector of the New Class which asserts the priority of its own cultural concerns over the purely technical and bureaucratic. It is thus the evolutionary, Fabian ideology of a kind of secular priesthood, primarily therapeutic and morally revitalizing in its basic intentions, rather than political.

*6.8 On Noam Chomsky:* If Shils stresses, indeed overemphasizes, the alienative disposition of intellectuals, Noam Chomsky denies they truly oppose the establishment and instead overstresses their subservience to power. Both, however, join in condemning the New Class, albeit for opposite reasons.

Chomsky is a scholar of immense moral authority (greatly justified) and of abounding moral energy (occasionally misplaced). In his Huizinga lecture he begins by citing approvingly Bakunin's condemnation of the reign of the New Class as aristocratic, despotic, arrogant, and elitist.[49] Yet one soon wonders why Chomsky cites Bakunin to this effect at all, since he himself does not believe that the New Class has any power. "Contrary to the illusions of post-industrial theorists," insists Chomsky, "power is not shifting into their hands."[50] Interestingly, Chomsky does not reject Bakunin's warning that the rule by socialist savants "is the worst of all despotic governments;" indeed, he seemingly finds this a not unfitting characterization of Soviet society. Apparently the reign of the New Class is imminent (and pernicious) in Soviet society, but merely chimerical in late capitalist society. Yet if the New Class is so inconsequential here, why spend time denouncing it; why not simply shrug it aside? Here Chomsky's position is not very clear.

Yet his recitation of the often shameless behavior of the New Class is convincing. Its toadying for favor, advancement, awards, and notice; its eagerness to provide (paid) services and arguments for both industry and the state; its readiness to be the "servant of power" (in Loren Baritz's apt phrase), are among the New Class's more unloveable traits. I can think of no epithet Chomsky uses that is altogether unjust.

Yet from another perspective it may be that these are simply characteristics common to rising groups before they take power. One wonders why Chomsky thinks the New Class should set a new historical standard of morality? In most societies most classes at most times serve the powers that be. Why shouldn't the New Class at first be the "servant of power"? The bourgeoisie, for example, was the servant of the court and crown for as long as it had to be. And the working class today is everywhere the servant of some power.

Chomsky apparently expects a higher moral standard from the New Class than from the others—but why? This implies that, for him, the trouble with the New Class is not that it is an elite but that it is not a *moral* elite. He is basically trying to "normalize" them, i.e. make them a *good* elite. Chomsky's critique of the New Class tacitly preaches that theirs (in Julian Benda's phrase) is a "treason of the clerics";[51] that is, he tacitly treats the New Class as priests *manquées*, and in this is reminiscent of Edward Shils.

Above all, Chomsky's standpoint is that of the moralist: noting, for example, that Charles Kadushin's study found that the American intellectual "elite" solidly opposed the Vietnamese War, Chomsky complains that they did not do so for the *right* reasons. They opposed it, he holds, on pragmatic grounds, out of a fear that the war could not be won, rather than out of high moral principle. The essence of the matter for Chomsky is that "the United States simply had no legal or moral right to intervene by force in the internal affairs of Vietnam."[52] I fully concur. From a moral point of view, however, would not one want to add, perhaps, that the Vietnamese in turn have no moral right to intervene in Cambodia (or the Cambodians in Vietnam)? And from an intellectual viewpoint, one should ask how the Vietnam policies of the intellectual elite *compared* with other American elites; for it seems likely that the intellectual elite was more opposed to the war, and more opposed for *moral* reasons, than *other* elites, political, military, economic. But this is a secular, comparative view of the intellectual elite, rather than one from the standpoint of eternity.

For Chomsky, even the most vigorous opponents of the system are really giving it secret help; for by their very public opposition, they imply that the system is democratic: "The more vigorous the debate, the better the system of propaganda is served. . . ."[53] Chomsky's position is grounded in the Marcusean thesis of the one-dimensionality of modern society which holds that even opposition to the system invigorates it. Such a view, aside from often being mistaken, also breeds political pessimism, social quietism and acquiescence to the *status quo*. The most effective achievements of American propaganda, concludes Chomsky, "are attributable to the method of feigned dissent practiced by the responsible intelligentsia."[54] Thus not only is the New Class aiding and abetting the system by their opposition to it, but their opposition is only a sham and pretense: "feigned." What this comes down to, then, is that the opponents of the system *can*not change it, while the system's friends do not *want* to. Thus no rational change is possible.

Yet the earth moves; the war was opposed, morally and effectively, and by the masses of the New Class. Chomsky's stress on feigned opposition obscures the real opposition. Perhaps the elite among intellectuals opposed the war primarily for pragmatic reasons, but most intellectuals were not members of that elite and often enough felt toward the war the very moral outrage that Chomsky prizes. If they are obscured in Chomsky's account, it is because they are dissonant with the picture he wants to draw of the New Class as singlemindedly devoted to the powers of the state and private industry, as the engineers of system-legitimation.

This creates a dilemma. What about those Chomsky cites favorably, such as David Noble's critique of engineers, *America by Design?* Or what of Christopher Lasch's critique of the welfare professions in his

*Haven in a Heartless World?* Is their opposition authentic or is it "feigned"? Better still, what of Chomsky himself? Is Chomsky's own opposition to the system or to the New Class specious and self-defeating? If not, how has he escaped the servile fate supposedly common to the New Class? To suggest he escapes is a tacit claim that he is a member of a rare elite superior to the ordinary New Class and, indeed, superior to the common run of mankind. Chomsky's position is thus elitist and self-contradictory. He cannot account for himself and for his own authentic resistance and effectiveness.

I would suggest, without in the least intending to deprecate Chomsky's very special contribution, that he is not so different from ordinary members of the New Class. He is simply *ahead* of them in the high, historical expectations he has of them. Indeed, his very capacity to mount a critique of the dominant system depends in part on his using the very code (CCD) *normal* to the New Class and which grounds its capacity, not only for a critique of the *status quo,* but also for the very reflexive *self*-criticism that Chomsky manifests.

My own conclusions: Chomsky moralizes too much. He spins a rationalist's picture of the social world as a seamless web, and his eager moralism is a vital part of his tacit elitism. Chomsky's very criticism of the New Class evidences their own familiar self-righteous elitism. His resistance to the system also exhibits the New Class's capacity to oppose the system, which resistance is as much a part of its social being as its subservience. The New Class is a contradictory class, but Chomsky's rationalism obscures these contradictions. At bottom, Chomsky is not the enemy of the New Class. He is its vanguard.

*6.9 Ecology and Systems Theory as New Class Ideologies:* Edward Shils and others have already indicated the lineaments of a history of New Class's ideologies: beginning with its Enlightenment component, such a history would go on to the Romantic reaction, to Positivistic scientism, to the fusion of Positivism and Romanticism in Marxism, and to the modern technological consciousness lineally descendent of Positivism (on which, more later). I have also noted the importance of "professionalism" as the New Class's central *occupational* ideology. Two newer forms of New Class's ideology are also emerging: environmentalism-ecology and general systems theory.

The new ecological ideology signifies that the older instrumental ideology of the New Class is giving way to one with keener concern for the goals of action and which refuses to surrender these to others and to limit itself to specifying the means of action. Its multi-science character provides an ideological framework that can unite various types of technical intelligentsia. At the same time its rejection of the idea of domination over nature, its intimation of a husbanding and indeed of a return to "nature," is also attractive to many humanistic intellectuals.

Like the new ecology, systems theory embodies a new vision of unity. But if ecology is grounded in organismic metaphor and has romantic antecedents, systems theory resonates a mechanical metaphor more continuous with the technocratic consciousness and, unlike ecology, embodies a humanistic imperialism centered on the impulse to manage (dominate) the environment. If ecology has a strong populistic tinge, systems theory is imbued with a stronger elitism, being "the 'natural' ideology of bureaucratic planners and centralizers . . ."[55]

Both ideologies, however, address themselves tacitly to the problem of the *dis*unity of the New Class, and may be understood as different efforts to bridge its various competing and divergent factions. Systems theory's elitism, however, narrows the social solidarity that it can foster, limiting it to the technical intelligentsia at best; ecology's capacity for fostering unity, while also grounded in a multi-science view, is, at least in some of its versions, open to a larger constituency and is potentially productive of a broader solidarity inclusive of humanistic no less than technical intelligentsia.

# Thesis Seven: Education and the Reproduction of the New Class

7.1 The necessary institution for the mass production of the New Class and its special culture of critical discourse is the historically unique system of "public education," whether at the secondary or tertiary levels. This system is characterized by the fact that (a) it is education *away from the home* and thus away from close parental supervision; (b) it is education mediated by a special group of New Class, "teachers," whose role invites them to take the standpoint of the collectivity as a whole, and who train students to believe that the value of their discourse does not depend upon their differing class origins, that it is not the speaker but the speech that is to be attended. (c) All public schools, therefore, are schools for a *linguistic conversion*, moving their charges *away from* the ordinary languages of their everyday lives and moving them toward the CCD.

7.2  The New Class is at first readied for contest against the old class by and in the new educational system. The public school system is increasingly separated from the family system. The training of the young is mediated by a *semi*-autonomous group of teachers speaking in the name of the nation or society "as a whole" and without any obligation to preserve a specific class's privileges. Students' ideologies and their parents' may now grow more divergent. Parents are now no longer able to reproduce the values of their class in their own children. Family values manifest more internal differences as mothers become more educated, allying themselves with the schools. With the school's functioning as a center of linguistic conversion to CCD, in which persons are trained not to justify assertions by invoking the speaker's social status, *all* authoritative claims are now *potentially open to challenge*. Parental, particularly paternal, authority is increasingly vulnerable and is thus less able to insist that children respect societal or political authority *outside* of the home. A grounding is established for the training of members of the New Class and for their alienation from the old class. Colleges and universities are the finishing schools of the New Class' resistance to the old class.

7.3  Schools, especially (but not only) tertiary schools, do as much and sometimes more to radicalize capitalist society than factories. It is school that is a major grounding for the alienation of the New Class. But how is this possible? Aren't schools, as Emile Durkheim, Herbert Marcuse and Louis Althusser[56] all agree, transmission belts for society's ruling values? Do they not teach the skills needed by the labor force and the attitudes of obedience necessary for the authority of the old class? Isn't the openness of schools simply a "repressive tolerance" that turns back all dissent, making it a tool for the reproduction of the *status quo?*

There is no doubt that schools and their faculties do much of that. Academicization often withdraws concern for the major crises of society, sublimating it into obsessive puzzle-solving, into "technical" interests. Obsequious professors may teach the advanced course in social cowardice, and specialists transmit narrow skills required by bureaucracies. But Ronald Reagan did not set out to curb the University of California because it was a servant of capitalism. And why the attack on CUNY (The City University of New York) if it, too, was only a servant of monopoly?

7.4 To understand modern universities and colleges we need an openness to contradiction. For universities both reproduce *and* subvert the larger society. We must distinguish between the functions universities publicly *promise* to perform—the social goods they are chartered to produce—and certain of their actual consequences which, while commonly unintended, are no less real: the production of dissent, deviance, and the cultivation of an authority-subverting culture of critical discourse.

An analogy: what could be more authoritarian than the Western patriarchal family? Aimed at reproducing its parents' and especially its father's values, it teaches submission, gratitude, obedience, loyalty; nonetheless, it also and unexpectedly produces: *Oedipus*, rebellion against the father. Like the patriarchal family, the school is surely conceived by its managers as an instrument for the self-perpetuation of the *status quo*. And yet, in both cases, while it rarely *teaches* rebellion, many young people learn it during their education. It is crucial to distinguish between what the institution sets out to *teach*, and what, by force of the conditions that exist, is actually *learned* there. While the school is designed to teach what is adaptive for the society's master institutions, it is also often hospitable to a culture of critical discourse by which authority is unwittingly undermined, deviance fostered, the *status quo* challenged, and dissent systematically produced.

7.5 With the growth of public education, the accumulation and distribution of cultural capital is now no longer so tightly correlated with moneyed capital. A New Class of the culturally advantaged is now created that is not as integrated with, and not as dependent on, the old class of the moneyed rich as it once was historically. Indeed, cultural capital increasingly controls resources requisite for the reproduction of moneyed capital, but the latter decreasingly controls the resources for the reproduction of cultural capital. Tertiary education, including the reproduction of the technical intelligentsia, even in capitalist countries, is now less dependent on the private sector and is increasingly dependent on the public sector or state. Some view this as the "socialization" of private industry's research and development costs—in other words, as a way the private sector transfers these costs to the public. This is correct, but it misses the contradictions in the situation. For in "socializing" such costs, the private sector loosens its control over the reproduction of the New Class and, increasingly, these become vested in the New Class itself.

7.6  Aside from incidental anecdote, is there any evidence at all that universities (at least sometimes) foster a culture of critical discourse? For a convenient summary, one may refer to Howard Bowen's recent and cautious sifting of a vast array of evidence on differences produced by going to college. Obviously, these various studies had not been conducted with my own interests in mind and can, therefore, be coordinated to my concerns here only in part, but treated carefully they are relevant. While this is not the place to add up the evidence, at least its availability should be noted.

For example, a study by Lehmann and Dressel found that critical thinking (including the recognition of unstated assumptions) "increased substantially over the four years, the gain being greater in the first two years of college than in the last two years."[57] Other studies by Feldman and Newcomb and by Heist and Yonge reported colleges as producing small increments in abstract reflective thought and theoreticity.[58] Various studies (e.g., Lehmann and Dressel and Spaeth and Greeley) have used self-assessments and "almost all indicate that an overwhelming majority of students and alumni believe they achieved considerable progress in . . . rationality during college."[59] Needless to say, such self-assessments surely cannot count as evidence of actually increased rationality, but they do imply that these persons *wish* to be thought of as having increased their rationality, suggesting that colleges may transform students' self-images or social identities in ways that might be rationality-enhancing. For similar reasons, it is notable that other studies have also found that upperclassmen and graduates believe college has furthered their ability to think critically, suggesting that, if not strengthening critical thinking, colleges may heighten the *value* students attribute to it.

It is particularly relevant to our notion of CCD (which, recall, rejects justification by authority) to note that many studies have found that college induces a decline in religiosity, a reduction in rigidity, authoritarianism, dogmatism, and ethnocentrism while increasing autonomy and complexity:

> The findings [of Feldman and Newcomb's 1969 appraisal of these studies] were so clear and striking that they require very little

explanation or interpretation. Almost every study revealed substantial increases in intellectual tolerance among college students
from the freshman to the senior year. . . . The results . . .
show a substantial decline in dogmatism. . . . [There were] substantial gains during college in Complexity, Nonauthoritarianism,
and Social Maturity . . . dramatic differences in gains for those
who attended college four years as compared to those who
dropped out of college, worked or became housewives. These
findings remained valid when controls for student ability levels
and socioeconomic status were introduced . . . gains in [intellec-
tual] tolerance are greater for students of the arts and sciences
than among those in such professional fields as business and engineering.[60]

Again, college education has been found, by studies from 1929 to
the 1960s, to *secularize* students: ". . . they indicate that students
become less favorable toward the church, less convinced of the reality
of God, less favorable toward observance of the Sabbath, less accepting of religious dogma . . . the greatest change occurring for those in
the liberal arts, and the least for those in professional fields."[61]

Again, and with respect to cosmopolitanism and language relevant
habits, it is found that "the better educated have wider and deeper
knowledge not only of bookish facts but also of many aspects of the
contemporary world. . . . There is [also] abundant evidence that
college alumni read more than high school graduates. They buy, own,
read more books. . . . These differences in reading habits persist
when the college and noncollege groups are stratified by income."[62]

Finally, apropos of the *reflexivity* that is critical for CCD, it is
notable that findings indicate that college attendance coincides with
increased self-awareness and self-openness: ". . . people with more
education seem to be more introspective about themselves, more
concerned about the personal and interpersonal aspects of their lives.
. . . The more highly educated respondents . . . seem to be more
aware of *both* the positive and the negative aspects of their
lives. . . ."[63]

# Thesis Eight: Intelligentsia and Intellectuals

8.1    There are at least two elites within the New Class: (1) *intelligentsia* whose intellectual interests are fundamentally "technical" and (2) *intellectuals* whose interests are primarily critical, emancipatory, hermeneutic and hence often political. Both elites utilize an elaborated linguistic variant and both are committed to the CCD. Both therefore resist the old class, although doing so in different ways in different settings and to different degrees.

While intellectuals often contribute to revolutionary leadership, they also serve to accommodate the future to the past and to reproduce the past in the future. That's what comes of the love of books. While the technical intelligentsia often wish nothing more than to be allowed to enjoy their opiate obsessions with technical puzzles, it is their social mission to revolutionize technology continually and hence disrupt established social solidarities and cultural values by never contenting themselves with the *status quo*. Revolutionary intellectuals are the medium of an ancient morality; accommodative intelligentsia are the medium of a new amorality. Which is more revolutionary?

8.2    The sociology and the social psychology of the occupational life of intellectuals and technical intelligentsia differ considerably, as do their cognitive procedures. Thomas Kuhn's notion of "normal science"[64] is a key to the cognitive life of technical intelligentsia and of their differences from intellectuals. A "normal science" is one whose members concentrate their efforts on solving the "puzzles" of "paradigms" on which normal science centers. Technical intelligentsia concentrate on operations within the paradigm(s) of their discipline, exploring its inner symbolic space, extending its principles to new fields, fine-tuning it. Intellectuals, in contrast, are those whose fields of activity more commonly lack consensually validated paradigms, may have several competing paradigms, and they therefore do not take normal science with its single dominating paradigm as the usual case. Intellectuals often transgress the boundaries of the conventional division of labor in intellectual life; they do not reject scholarship, however, but only the *normalization* of scholarship.

8.3 It would be tempting but far too simple to say, intellectuals produce the "lions" of the New Class, while the intelligentsia produce its "foxes." Who is a lion and who a fox depends on whose way upward is being blocked. Where recruitment of college teachers is under the close control of the national ministry, as for example in Israel, members of the Israeli Communist Party and any who seem well disposed toward it have little chance of being hired.[65] In parts of the Mid-East, then, it is often the case that teachers and other intellectuals are relatively prudent politically, while doctors, engineers, and lawyers—being "independent"—may be more openly radical. Che Guevara, it will be remembered, was a doctor, as is George Habash; Yasir Arafat was trained as an engineer.

# Thesis Nine: Old Line Bureaucrats, New Staff Intelligentsia

9.1 With the growth of the technical intelligentsia, the functional autonomy of the old class wanes. The intelligentsia of the New Class manage the new means of production and administration; they also acquire at-hand control over the new means of communication and of *violence*. If we think of the state's repressive apparatus within the framework of Marxism there is no way to explain the recent revolutions in Ethiopia and Portugal, where the military played a singular role. In less developed countries, military intelligentsia are often the vanguard of the New Class.

Marxism misses the paradox that the old class can influence the state, or any other administrative system for that matter, only with the mediation of the New Class. It is not simply a matter of the split between "management and ownership" within capitalism, first, because that split is no less true of "socialism," and secondly, because the split is not confined to the production of commodities, but also includes the production of *violence*. As the organizational units of the economy and state become larger and more bureaucratic, the survival and control of the old class becomes more attenuated, more indirect, ever more dependent on the intelligentsia of the New Class.

9.2   The fundamental organizational instrument of our time, the bureaucratic organization, becomes increasingly scientized. The old bureaucratic officials at first provide a protective cover for the growth of the New Class. But as the number and importance of technical experts operating with CCD increases, there is a growing split between the old line bureaucrats and the technical intelligentsia. It becomes ever more difficult even for those *managing* the organization simply to understand the skills of the New Class, let alone to exert an ongoing, close control over them. The bureaucratic organization, as the dominant organizational type of the modern era, is controlled by an uneasy coalition of three elements: (i) top managing directors appointed from outside the bureaucracy and who do not usually control the technical expertise of the New Class or the complex details known to bureaucratic officials, (ii) New Class experts, and (iii) bureaucratic "line" officials whose modes of rationality differ.[66]

9.3   The cadre of the *old* bureaucratic structure are an officialdom, "bureaucrats," who ground their orders in terms of their legal *authority:* "do this because *I* say so, and I am authorized to say so." They are the *older* elite of the bureaucracy, the "bureaucrats" of legendary stigma, the "line" officials whose position depends simply on their rigorous conformity with organizational rules, obedience to their superiors' orders, the legality of their appointment, and sheer seniority. Their principal function is *control* over the behavior of those beneath them and those outside the organization. They are rooted in the elemental impulse of domination. In short, they are the organization's old "snake brain."

Having no reasons he can speak, the bureaucratic official does not justify his actions by arguing that they contribute to some desirable goal. He simply says he is conforming with the rules which, as Max Weber noted, he treats as "a basis of action for their own sake"; in the sinister phrase, he is "following orders." Either way, he serves as a transmission belt. He is passing on orders or policies that he is expected to obey whatever his personal feeling and whether or not he agrees with them.

These orders or policies are, then, placed beyond the domain of the culture of critical discourse. The old bureaucratic official was designed to be an "agent," uncritically obedient to the organization's top *managers* who, in turn, transmit the ideological and economic interests of social groups outside of the bureaucracy, and who are appointed because they can be relied upon to do just that. Bureaucratic officials are the agents of an internal colonialism, the instruments of an Indirect Rule. The bureaucratic officialdom are the brute part of bureaucracy, the barriers by which the technical intelligentsia are caged, and at the same time they are the protective covering for the New Class's first growth within the bureaucracy.

9.4 Unlike the older bureaucrats, the new intelligentsia have extensive cultural capital which increases their mobility. The old bureaucrat's skills are often little more than being able to read, write, file, and are limited to their employing bureaucracy. The new intelligentsia's greater cultural capital is, indeed, *more productive of goods and services* and they are, therefore, less concerned to vaunt their personal superiority or to extract deference from those below them. As a result, the old bureaucrats and the new intelligentsia develop and reproduce different systems of social control. Bureaucrats employ a control apparatus based on "ordering and forbidding," threatening and punishing the disobedient or resistant. The intelligentsia of the New Class, capable of increasing services and production, typically seek to control by *rewarding* persons for conformity to their expectations, by providing more material incentives and, also, by educational indoctrination. The intelligentsia of the New Class is a task-centered and work-centered elite having considerable confidence in its own worth and its future and, correspondingly, has less status anxiety that they irrationally impose on others. They are less overbearing and less punishment-prone. They need not, moreover, seek status solely within their own organization and from its staff or clients. Rather, they also seek status in professional associations; they wish the good regard of the knowledgeable.

9.5 The technical intelligentsia of the New Class is controlled by those incompetent to judge its performances and whose control, therefore, is experienced as irrational.[67] The New Class intelligentsia, then, feel a certain contempt for their superiors; for they are not competent participants in the careful discourse concerning which technical decisions are made. The New Class's intelligentsia are controlled by two echelons above them: one, the *bureaucratic officialdom*, the "line officials," *directly* above them; two, the *political* appointees managing the bureaucracy at its pinnacle, who are not appointed on the basis of their technical competence, but because they represent money capital or politically reliable "commissars." The fundamental structure within which most technical intelligentsia work, then, systematically generates tensions between them, on the one side, and the bureaucratic officials and managers, on the other. It is within the bureaucratic structure that much of the technical intelligentsia of the New Class begins its struggle to rise. It has one of its first muffled confrontations with the old class within the precincts of a specific organizational structure, the bureaucracy.

9.6   By comparison with line bureaucrats, the technical intelligentsia of the New Class are veritable philosophers. By comparison with the intellectuals, the intelligentsia may seem *idiots savants*. In contrast to the bureaucrats, however, the intelligentsia seeks nothing for its own sake, gives reasons without invoking authority, and regards nothing as settled once for all. To them, nothing is exempt from re-examination. Unlike the bureaucrats, intelligentsia are not "ritualists" pursuing something without regard to its effectiveness.

9.7   At the same time, however, nothing is sacred to them; their primary concern is with the technical effectiveness of their means rather than its moral propriety. They are pragmatic nihilists. They are capable of emancipating men from old shibboleths, but they are emancipators who know no limits. Their emancipation has a side effect: cultural destructiveness, *anomie*. The cultural dissolution they bring is precisely that always entailed by the culture of critical discourse, which commonly alienates persons from tradition.[68] In short, *like intellectuals, the intelligentsia, too, are a revolutionary force*. But the revolutionary power of the technical intelligentsia of the New Class is dammed-up by the bureaucratic barrier and the old form of property.

9.8   If the technical sub-elite of the New Class have the makings of a "benign" elite, they nonetheless remain an *elite*. They have no intention of instituting a social order in which all are *equal* regardless of their cultural capital. They do not think of themselves as an "intellectual proletariat," let alone as an ordinary proletariat. Contributing to the increase of the social surplus by the increased productivity of their cultural capital, they will benignly increase the funds available for welfare, may even accept worker participation in setting incentives, increase consumerism, even increasing job security. Although seeking it for themselves, they do not tolerate "workers' control" and they do not believe in equality.[69] Talk of "workers' control" is for the most part produced by a different sector of the New Class, by radicalized *intellectuals*, and not the technical intelligentsia.

9.9   Maoism was essentially an effort to avoid the resurgence of the old line bureaucratic officials *and* of the technical intelligentsia of the New Class. But the intelligentsia is the more rational elite, increasing both social productivity and social understanding, and now China is liquidating the "cultural revolution" and opting for the New Class.[70] Distilled to essentials, Maoism was an effort to strengthen the bargaining position of the working class (including the peasantry) in its inescapable, forthcoming negotiations with the New Class. For its part, and unlike Maoism, Stalinism was a profoundly regressive force because it sought to subordinate the technical intelligentsia to the most archaic sector, the old bureaucratic officialdom.[71]

As the old class deteriorates and loses control, especially with the rise of state socialism, the real choices are between the new technical intelligentsia and the old line bureaucrats. And it *is* a real choice. The rule of the bureaucratic officialdom is callous and authoritarian, while the rule of the new cultural elite, able to increase the level of productivity, can rely more on rewards than punishment and on the demystified performance of tasks without the mystique of authority or the extortion of personal deference.

# Thesis Ten: Revolutionary Intellectuals

It is fitting to begin these theses on the revolutionary politics of intellectuals with certain remarks by Fidel Castro: "To be quite honest, we must admit that, often before now, when it came to crucial issues, to imperialist aggression and crime, it was the intellectual workers who showed the greatest militancy, who reacted with the greatest determination, and not those political organizations whom one might in all conscience, have expected to give the lead."[72] The occasion of these observations was Castro's remarkable speech in Havana, January 1968, before the Cultural Congress on the role of intellectuals in the revolution. Castro's remarks imply much of the argument to be proposed by the theses below.

*10.1* That learned Marxist historian, Eric Hobsbawm, tells us plainly and correctly that during the Russian Revolution, "the leadership of the Bolsheviks consisted overwhelmingly of intellectuals, as did that of all other popular parties of opposition." Of the 25 members of the Politburo of the Russian Communist Party from 1919 to 1950–51 (and of whose education we know), nine had a university education, two went to seminaries, and six to high schools. But note also, this is probably biassed against the reporting of advanced education by communist leaders; note, too, that this sample includes the Stalin years, when intellectuals were hardly in favor. There is no doubt that the top ranks of the Old Bolsheviks consisted overwhelmingly of intellectuals, who were middle class in origin, well travelled, and who read broadly and wrote extensively. The average member of the early Politburo undoubtedly wrote more books than the average economics professor. Even Stalin wrote several books which, he saw to it, had numerous readers. The early Bolsheviks were dominated by intellectuals who evidently believed in the rule, publish or perish. Stalin later taught them another rule, publish *and* perish.

*10.2* Throughout the Third World, as the Austro-Marxist Franz Marek argued, "it is the intellectual elite who show the peasants how to organize and do the organizing." Mao tells us he was the "scholar of his family." Chou En-lai studied in China, Japan, France, and Germany. Chu Teh, together with Chou En-lai, also studied in Europe. Liu Shao-ch'i studied advanced economics in the USSR. Of the 29 Politburo members of the Chinese Communist Party from its inception until 1965, only two had no higher education; only two had only a Chinese education; 25 of the 29 studied in some foreign country.[73] Leadership of the Chinese Communist Party began with Ch'en Tu-hsiu who taught at Peking University and who, with the chief librarian there, Li Ta-chao, began organizing socialists a year after the Russian Revolution. One of the first projects of Ch'en was to organize the School of Foreign Languages in Shanghai to ready young radicals to study abroad.

*10.3* The revolutionary elite in Vietnam unmistakably resembles that in China in the leading role played by intellectuals: "In tradi-

tional Vietnam the leadership of wars of resistence against foreign
invaders was provided by Confucian scholars who had remained in
their villages instead of accepting official posts as mandarins. . . . In
time honored fashion, scholars led the first sustained resistance to the
French, the *Van Than* (Scholars' Resistance) and *Can Vuong* (Loyalty
to the King) Movements of 1885–97. . . . The heroic words and
deeds of that period were added to tales of earlier scholar-led up-
risings."[74]

The dominant figure of the Vietnamese Revolution, Ho Chi Minh,
was the son of a talented Confucian scholar thought to have taken part
in the Scholars' Resistance. After having been Minister of Rites at the
Imperial Palace in Hue in 1905, Ho's father was subsequently dis-
missed by the French for his nationalism, and Ho's family was thrust
into poverty. The father of Vo Nguyen Giap, Hanoi's leading military
strategist, was a poor scholar who had also participated in the
Scholars' Resistance. The family histories of many other leaders of the
Vietnamese Revolution show that the sons of scholars and mandarins
had a special part, particularly if their fathers were nationalists who
had resisted the French. Clearly, revolution is often a two generation
project; of young revolutionaries, it may often be said, as the Old Tes-
tament did: "The fathers have eaten of sour grapes and the teeth of
the children are set on edge."

As in China, many young Vietnamese revolutionaries received
their educations abroad, particularly in Japan and France. From 1905
on, a leading Confucian scholar, Phan Boi Chau, had arranged for
young Vietnamese—mostly sons of those in the Scholars' Resistance—to study in Japan. This was the *Gung Du*, or Eastern Study
movement which ended when French pressure led to their expulsion
from Japan. Chau, a frequent visitor to Ho's house, wanted Ho's father to send him to Japan for study, but the father, believing French
more practical, sent him to the first Vietnamese high school that com-
bined Vietnamese with Western education. The educational facilities
that Ho organized later in his life were no less important than those
earlier made available to him. Thus while Ho was with Borodin's
Comintern staff in Canton in 1924, he organized and taught a special
course on Revolution, whose students were later to become the Indo-
Chinese Communist Party's earliest Politburo.

*10.4* The revolution in Cambodia was also grounded in a fusion of
peasantry and intellectuals, under the tutelage of exceptionally ascetic
intellectuals. Some military cadre of its communist movement, the
Khmer Rouge, were trained in Hanoi after 1954. After 1959, they

were joined by increasing numbers of French educated Phnom Penh intellectuals disillusioned with their city's corruption.[75] Among early arrivals were radicalized teachers such as Ieng Sary, Saloth Sar, and Son Senn. A later arrival was Ieng Thirith, who has a diploma in Shakespearian studies.

After the peasant revolt in Battambang was put down in a bloody way by Sihanouk (a revolt in which communist military forces had helped), other left intellectuals fled Phnom Penh, among them Khieu Samphan, who joined the leadership of the new communist regime. Samphan had written a doctorate on the problems of industrializing Cambodia as a university student in Paris in the 1950s. The ingredients in the Cambodian Revolution were classic: an aroused and bloodied peasantry ready to join guerilla forces under the guidance of a highly educated intellectual elite, whose ascetic impulses are aggravated by the corruption of an old regime which they identified with the city. An additional element is added in the form of a hinterland, Vietnam, from whom they at first receive military training, and equipment, as well as refuge.

*10.5 Addendum:*   Note that those mentioned above (in China, Vietnam, Russia, or Cambodia) are *communists*, not socialists. It is everywhere the case that the preponderance of the New Class in the leadership of socialist parties is even greater than in communist parties. The leadership of the socialists in the United States, for example, during the party's zenith prior to World War I, was largely recruited from lawyers, editors, journalists, and teachers. They recruited heavily, as one of their leaders, Morris Hillquit (journalist and lawyer) said, "from the better classes. . . ." It is also true that the New Class has provided the central cadres for modern terrorists such as the Baader-Meinhoff group in Germany, the "Red Army" faction in Japan, the Red Brigades in Italy, the United States, and much of Latin America.

*10.6* The mandarin character of revolutionaries began with Marx and Engels themselves, and with the left Hegelians from whom they emerged. The left Hegelians were scholars of middle class origins who, emphasizes Goran Therborn,[76] were characteristically "nonbohemian." In other words: bourgeois. Who could have been more bourgeois than Marx who tyranically grilled his daughters' suitors, demanding assurance that they would not be kept in the poverty in which he had reared them. And who more mandarin than the Marx

who knew his Goethe by heart, who read his Aeschylus in the original, whose respect for Shakespeare was boundless, who read two or
three novels at one time, who took refuge in algebra as others do in
crossword puzzles, and who actually wrote an infinitesimal calculus.
"I am," he wrote his daughter Laura in 1868, ". . . a machine condemned to devour books. . . ."

Marx and Marxism are the creations of a library-haunting, book-
store-browsing, museum-loving—and hence leisure-possessing—
academic intelligentsia. They are unthinkable without the entire pan-
oply of libraries, bookstores, journals, newspapers, publishing
houses, even party schools, whose cadre and culture constitute a
dense infra-structure at whose center there is the Western university.

10.7 A Postscript: "And what of Engels?" we will be asked. Since
Engels never went to University, isn't he a negative instance? Not exactly. He did spend a year at the University of Berlin, while doing his
tour of duty with the Household Regiment, where he attended lec-
tures from no less than Schelling. More startling still were the names
of his fellow auditors: Kierkegaard, Burckhardt, Bakunin. With such a
gathering of eagles, who needs professors! But not too fast, there was
one other great professor who gave Engels a life-long personal tutorial
session: yes, exactly. . . .

# Thesis Eleven: The Alienation of
# Intellectuals and Intelligentsia

11.1 The term *intelligenty* was used in Russia during the 1860s to
refer to a self-conscious elite of the well educated characterized by
critical tendencies toward the *status quo;* the term "intellectuals"
came into vogue through the "Manifesto of Intellectuals" protesting
the French government's persecution of Dreyfuss.

The alienative disposition of intellectuals and intelligentsia is thus
by no means recent, even though my focus is on its manifestations in
the twentieth century. Seymour Lipset and Asoke Basu remind us
that

Luther's revolt against the church found its initial support from
the faculty and students of his University at Wittenberg and elsewhere in Germany. . . . Hobbes, writing of the causes of the
English Revolution in Behemoth concluded that the universities
were the principal source of the rebellion. . . . In Russia the
various revolutionary movements were intellectual and student
based until the Revolution of 1905. That revolt began with a
student strike which subsequently spread to the workers and sections of the peasantry.[77]

11.2    What are the origins of the alienation of the New Class? To ask
a different question first: how did Marx and Engels account for the
radicalization of classes other than the proletariat? In short: how do
they account for *themselves?*

They remark: ". . . the communist consciousness . . . may, of
course, arise among other classes, too, through the contemplation of
the situation of (the working) class."[78] *The Communist Manifesto*
has equally unenlightening remarks: ". . . when the class struggle
nears the decisive hour . . . a small section of the ruling class cuts itself adrift and joins the revolutionary class . . . and, in particular, a
portion of the bourgeois ideologists who have raised themselves to
the level of comprehending theoretically the historical movement as a
whole."[79] According to Marx and Engels, then, some intellectuals are
radicalized by their "contemplation" and *theoretical* comprehension
of history. It is striking how *idealistic* Marx and Engels' account of the
process is. Clearly, this contradicts Marxism's fundamental assumption that "social being determines consciousness." How could the
consciousness of a revolutionary proletariat emerge among those
whose social being was that of the "ruling class"? Marx and Engels'
fugitive remarks about intellectuals signal that *Marxism has here
abruptly reached the limits of its self-understanding.* What Marx and
Engels have given, in answer to this fundamental question, is really a
silence concealed by a gloss.

11.3    Putting aside their idealistic gloss, how do we account for the
alienation of intellectuals and intelligentsia? In terms of: (a) the culture
of critical discourse (CCD), which does not focus on *what* intellectuals
think about but on *how* they think; (b) the blockage of their opportunities for upward mobility; (c) the disparity between their income and
power, on the one side, and their cultural capital and self-regard, on
the other; (d) their commitment to the social totality; (e) the contradictions of the technical, especially the blockage of their technical interests.

In important part, the culture of critical discourse constitutes the characterizing values of the New Class; the other considerations (b-e) bear on the question of whether and how far the New Class will *adhere* to the *CCD*. To ignore the role of values in shaping a group's behavior is vulgar materialism; to omit analysis of the conditions under which persons conform with or deviate from their values is vulgar idealism.

*11.4* CCD is radicalizing partly because, as a relatively situation-free speech variant, it experiences itself as distant from (and superior to) ordinary languages and conventional cultures. A relatively situation-free discourse is conducive to a *cosmopolitanism* that distances persons from local cultures, so that they feel an alienation from all particularistic, history-bound places and from ordinary, everyday life.

The grammar of critical discourse claims the right to sit in judgment over the actions and claims of any social class and all power elites. From the standpoint of the culture of critical discourse, all claims to truth, however different in social origin, are to be judged in the same way. Truth is democratized and all truth claims are now equal *under* the scrutiny of CCD. The claims and self-understanding of even the most powerful group are to be judged no differently than the lowliest and most illiterate. Traditional authority is stripped of its ability to define social reality and, with this, to authorize its own legitimacy. The "credit" normally given to the claims of the rich and powerful now becomes a form of deviant, illicit behavior that needs to be hidden if not withdrawn.

*11.5* Notice, then, that CCD treats the relationship between those who speak it, and others *about whom* they speak, as a relationship between judges and judged. It implies that the established social hierarchy is only a semblance and that the deeper, more important distinction is between those who speak and understand truly and those who do not. To participate in the culture of critical discourse, then, is to be emancipated *at once* from lowness in the conventional social hierarchy, and is thus a subversion of that hierarchy. To participate in the culture of critical discourse, then, is a political act.

*11.6* Indeed, it is not only subversion of the present, but a "revolution-in-permanence" that is grounded in the culture of critical discourse. The essence of critical discourse is in its insistence on reflexivity. There is the obligation to examine what had hitherto been taken for granted, to transform "givens" into "problems," resources into topics: to examine the life we lead, rather than just enjoy or suffer it. It is therefore not only the present but also the anti-present, the *critique* of the present and the assumptions it uses, that the culture of critical discourse must also challenge. In other words: the culture of critical discourse must put its hands around its own throat, and see how long it can squeeze. CCD always moves on to auto-critique, *and* to the critique of *that* auto-critique. There is an unending regress in it, a potential revolution in permanence; it embodies that unceasing restlessness and "lawlessness" that the ancient Greeks first called *anomos* and that Hegel had called the "bad infinity."

It is, therefore, fitting that Leon Trotsky, proponent of The Permanent Revolution, should have been uneasy about the revolution he himself had made and that he rejected "socialism in one country." It was not just Trotsky's momentary politics and concrete policies that Stalinism rejected—indeed, it later took some of these over—but the entire culture of critical discourse on which these had been based. Trotskyism represented the refusal of CCD and its critique to let things simmer down.[80]

*11.7* The alienation of the New Class of intellectuals (and intelligentsia) is based also on the blockage of their upward mobility. The first political appearance of radicalized intellectuals in politics, the Jacobin leadership, was in part prompted by the fact that their careers had at first manifested upward mobility, but their future ascendance was blocked by aristocratic preemptions; they were "blocked ascendants,"[81] not *déclassés*.

A somewhat similar phenomenon has been noticed in Third World countries where, to meet their manpower needs, foreign invaders set up schools and train a select group of native intellectuals whose number, however, soon exceeds the career chances open to them.[82] A trained and articulate elite of dimmed prospect (except that provided by revolution) is thus created. Such career blockages are not, however, peculiar to less developed Third World countries but are found also in the "first" and "second" worlds. The emerging oversupply of Ph.D.'s and other educated manpower in Western Europe and the United States (on which, more later) is structurally similar. Again, limitations placed on the careers of the native intelligentsia in colonialized republics of the USSR have a similar import. For example, Donald Carlisle's study of Uzbek Soviet intelligentsia observes that "today in the ranks of the Party and the intelligentsia in the Uzbek SSR, Russians continue to play a large and key role out of proportion to their share of the local population." Will ethnic and nationalist tensions unfold, asks Carlisle, "as more and more Uzbeks emerge from the schools armed with skills but confronted by Russians and Ukrainians blocking the channels for mobility and occupying key positions?" [83]

A nationalist movement against foreign imperialisms is, among other things, a struggle to preempt elite positions for *native* intellectuals and intelligentsia, by taking over and creating their own state apparatus. The creation of their own state apparatus is a way the native New Class advantages its own elite culture. The crucial obstacle to Third World intellectuals in colonized countries are *foreign* imperialists. In the First World of capitalism, however, it is the old class of moneyed property which sets the ultimate limits on the New Class. It is the local, "internal colonists" of the old class who are the last obstacle to the ascendence of the New Class.

Socialism is the final removal of that limit. In collectivizing the means of production the power of the moneyed old class is destroyed. In transferring the means of production to *state* control, thus swelling the bureaucratic apparatus of the state, socialism extends the domain within which the New Class's cultural capital holds sway. It is precisely because control of the means of production by the *state* is a mechanism advantaging the New Class that this is supported by them rather than democratizing the means of production. Socialism, then, is a way of extending the New Class's cultural capital—that is, enlarging the sphere within which its cultural capital is assured incomes. The decisive mark of socialism is elimination of moneyed capital, the old class; its inevitable consequence, however recognized or unintended, is to pave the way for cultural capital; i.e., for the New Class.

*11.8 On the State: A Slightly Expanded Model:* The basic process here is the extension of the state: indeed, the development of socialism itself becomes, from this standpoint, a special case of, or special occasion for, the extension of the state. There are several stages:

*Stage One.* A nationalist or anti-imperialist movement emerges. This implies two things: (a) extension of the new state's bureaucracy and (b) making the new bureaucracy a monopoly of the indigenous New Class.

*Stage Two.* The extended production of the New Class: the state expands the school system and with this the number of trained members of the New Class.

*Stage Three.* Overproduction of the New Class.

*Stage Four.* The socialist adaptation: here the point is that socialism entails an extension of the functions of the state and, with this, a further extension of bureaucratic opportunities for the New Class.

Often the nationalist and socialist forces are fused—as anti-imperialism—and brought together in time and under a single movement. One reason this is possible is that both nationalism and socialism have a common programmatic implication—extension of the state.

*11.9*  The importance of blocked ascendence for revolutionary intellectuals was visible in the Parisian leadership of the Jacobins, but it scarcely began there. Blocked ascendence is found also in the leadership of the American Revolution. Relative to the old class and men of moneyed property, the New Class of intellectuals and intelligentsia are in general blocked ascendents. Being relatively well educated, the New Class has by that fact alone already begun its upward mobility. Although prompted by all manner of considerations to better themselves in the world, the New Class of cultural bourgeoisie are inherently limited in what they can aspire to. Under capitalism, they are limited by property; under state socialism, by the Party and its requirements of ideological certification (i.e., being "red"). The generic impulse of those intellectuals seeking socialism is to eliminate the bourgeoisie of property, the old class, which is the most immediate block to their own continuing ascendency. It is, after all, easier to join the party than to join the bourgeoisie.

*11.10*  Blocked ascendence appears to have been an important factor both in the American Revolution, and in the formation of the Russian *intelligenty* who played so significant a role in the several Russian Revolutions. Of the Russian *intelligenty,* Aleksander Gella remarks that it developed in a "state where all important governmental positions were occupied by the aristocracy (and) consisted, to a vastly larger extent than in Poland, of people of the lower classes, for example, minor officials." It is known that the leaders of the American Revolution were more likely to have been college educated than was the general public at that time: "Education produced high expectations in men who as youngsters had not enjoyed more than their share of scarce socioeconomic rewards—with each new economic or political accomplishment they expected more success and recognition. Yet the pattern of prerevolutionary political immobility cut such men off from the highest offices and the greatest chance for colony-wide and intercolonial political standing."[84]

' Part of what had produced the American Revolution, then, was this: colonial leaders could only aspire to seats in the lower houses of Assemblies, and since this was the locus of their power, they made the Assemblies as autonomous as possible. After indifference to this development for almost a century, however, the Crown and Parliament began to restrict the autonomy of the Assemblies: "With no prospect of political mobility above the Assembly level, many of them saw no reason to hand back what they had taken away from their opponents in higher offices."[85] They became the adversaries of the higher officials and of the Crown who had appointed them, declaring that what was being done to the Assemblies was only a forerunner of what would happen to the liberties of all Americans. This pattern, namely, the British reassertion of rights and powers that had eroded through their earlier neglect, is also reminiscent of conditions prior to the French Revolution, where some of the aristocracy had also sought to reassert ancient prerogatives they had allowed to wane.

*11.11*  Blocked ascendence produces an increase in the *political* activity by the New Class and in open acts of confrontation with authority, not only when the economic interests of intellectuals are restricted but, also when their opportunities to exercise *political* influence are blocked. The impairment of the New Class's upward mobility, either *politically or economically*, contributes to their alienation. Thus Charles Kadushin's study of the elite intellectual in the United States during the Vietnam War found that his political activity varied, depending in part on "whether or not he had a direct line to men of power—if he did, he was less likely to engage in demonstrations and never engaged in civil disobedience. . . ."[86]

*11.12*  Note the lines of communication initiated by the New Class concerning public problems: in a late-capitalist society such as the United States, when leaders of the New Class want to affect national outcomes and to influence men of power, they communicate with *politicians* at the national level, i.e., with "Washington." They do *not* initiate direct communication with the old class, i.e., with business leaders. This implies that they do not invest their hopes in the policies or actions of business leaders, and no longer view them as effective or legitimate leaders of the *nation*.

Although the early "utopian" socialists, Charles Fourier and Henri Saint-Simon, had solicited help from rich industrialists, the latter's jealous disciple and founder of Positivism, Auguste Comte, was soon disillusioned and abandoned hope in businessmen, as his letters suggest.[87]

*11.13*   The central *mode* of influence used by and characteristic of the New Class is *communication*—writing and talking. Unlike the old class, they do not *buy* conformity with their interests but seek to *persuade* it. Unlike politicians, they normally do not have *force* available to impose their goals. The New Class gets what it wants, then, primarily by rhetoric, by persuasion and argument through publishing or speaking.

The political and economic interests of the New Class, then, are uniquely dependent on their continuing access to media, particularly mass media, and upon institutional freedoms protecting their right to publish and speak. Impairment of these rights—that is, censorship—is a basic liability in the New Class's effort to advance itself. Since its ascendence depends greatly on its access to free communication, its opposition to censorship is one of the main struggles that has *united* it historically, as in the period prior to the French Revolution, and even today. Indeed, New Class opposition to censorship cross cuts both East and West; it is now an important source of the alienation of the Soviet intelligentsia, as the rise of the *samizdat* indicate. One may note that it is here, in its opposition to censorship, that the partisan class interests of the New Class coincide with universal interests in public rationality.

*11.14*   At the beginnings of bourgeois society, tensions between the emerging New Class and the bourgeoisie were commonly inhibited because of their joint opposition to the Old Regime which had subjected them to a common repression, limiting them both in the pursuit of their interests. Having a common enemy, they could make a common cause. It was the common interests of both classes that were rationalized and universalized by the Enlightenment. Censorship was a powerful grievance activating intellectuals to become the universalizing agency of bourgeois property.

The universalization of the struggle against the Old Regime was in part a resistance to the latter's linguistic repression, i.e., to its censorship and to its restriction of intellectuals' freedom to publish and to realize an income from their writing. The bourgeois revolution was commonly based on an alliance between the propertied and the educated sections of the middle class—the bourgeoisie and the intellectuals. The bourgeois revolution was grounded therefore in a highly *transient* situation in which both literary property and the other forms of bourgeois property, being subjected to a common oppression, were united. This historic alliance was soon severed as the *propertied* part of the middle class won power in the state and economy, increasing its control over the educated part of the middle class. Economic power begins to replace state censorship as the object of the intellectuals' hostility; their contempt for "philistinism" expresses the transition from state censorship to "censorship" by the market place.

11.15 A third source of the alienation of the New Class is their experience of a status disparity, a disparity between their great possession of culture and their correspondingly lesser enjoyment of incomes in power and wealth. *Humanistic intellectuals* (i.e., a section of the New Class) in a technocratic industrial society experience an especially sharp status disparity between their "high" culture and their more limited incomes or political influence, and they grow increasingly alienated. Intellectuals and intelligentsia may both become alienated when their form of capital brings a lower return, in power and wealth, than the incomes of the moneyed capital of the old class.

The New Class believes its high culture represents the greatest achievement of the human race, the deepest ancient wisdom and the most advanced modern scientific knowledge. It believes that these contribute to the welfare and wealth of the race, and that they should receive correspondingly greater rewards. The New Class believes that the world should be governed by those possessing superior competence, wisdom and science—that is, themselves. The Platonic Complex, the dream of the philosopher king with which Western philosophy begins, is the deepest wish-fulfilling fantasy of the New Class. But they look around and see that the men who employ them do not begin to understand the simplest aspects of their technical specialties, and that the politicians who rule them are, in Edmund Wilson's words, "unique in having managed to be corrupt, uncultivated, and incompetent all at once." [88]

11.16 A fourth source of the alienation of the New Class is their concern for and commitment to the social "totality." Their privileged education and the social roles they play are often defined as entailing an obligation to the collectivity as a whole. Teachers, for example, are commonly defined as "representatives" of the *whole* society and guardians of its national traditions. Indeed, even some of the old classes, particularly traditional elites, may feel a responsibility for the group as a whole.

In colonial situations, displaced traditional elites are sometimes disposed by their class interests and their culture, to take leadership against the foreigners corrupting their society's traditions; they have sometimes been trained to take the standpoint of the totality as a matter of *noblesse oblige*. Even if seeing it from a unique perspective, i.e., from the top down, they may achieve a coherent picture of the whole society and develop a feeling of obligation to it. However false such a consciousness may be, it is often real in its consequences, leading some to be alienated from those elites, when they define them as self-seeking and corrupt or ineffectual[89] in protecting the larger groups' interests from foreigners.

11.17 Fifth and last among the sources of the New Class' alienation is the blockage of its technical interests. The subservience of technicians is often seen as due only to their venality, ambition, timidity. But it is these only in part. There is also their own lotus-eating nature. As Nietzsche once said, they are mushroom pickers, devoted to their own little puzzles and compulsions. Given the chance, they will support those who support their "habit." Their compulsive-obsessive involvement in the technical may make them apolitical, but there is a limit to this apoliticism. They can ignore politics and policy only so long as they can indulge their narcotizing technical obsessions. Once blocked in this, they, too, enter into contention with their bureaucratic superiors. Their very commitment to technical interests generates dissonance with their superiors who seek to prevent their pursuit of problems promising no practical payoffs. Inherent in a technical interest, then, is not simply subservience and the reproduction of the power *status quo* but also potential subversion of it. Even from the standpoint of their own limited instrumental rationality, technical intelligentsia find the world too little rational. Flawed though this rationality is, it regards itself as superior to the rationality of their bureaucratic superiors. And it is.

11.18 *Overproduction of Educated Manpower, New Class Unity, and Alienation:* Of the five sources of alienation mentioned above, one promises to intensify sharply the alienation of the New Class in the near future *and to heighten its internal unity against the old class.*

(We return here, for the third and last time, to the problem of the "unity" of the New Class.) This factor is an intensification of *blocked ascendence* brought about by the growing oversupply of educated manpower that became visible in the late 1960s. We have now entered a period in which there may be more educated manpower than demand for it; more unemployment among the New Class; increased pressure on them to accept jobs they do not want; and, consequently, increased job dissatisfaction among those working. The former upward mobility of the New Class, which had experienced growing prospects from the 1940s to the 1960s is now being blocked. The educated, who had commonly manifested higher than average job-satisfaction, may soon show that frustrated higher expectations induce sharper alienation.

Structurally, this developing glut of educated manpower is essentially similar to that found in colonial countries where it was a classic source of the emergence of anti-imperialist movements for national independence, and especially of their leadership. The developing oversupply of the educated has now spread to industrialized countries where it has become one important source of political radicalism, and even of armed terrorism, among educated youths. While the most active leaders of such groups are often motivated by ideological considerations, their following is frequently among educated youths without job prospects. There is reason to believe that these structural factors will also produce their usual consequences in the United States, Japan, France, Italy, and other industrial countries.

In 1973, the Carnegie Commission on Higher Education predicted that the supply of educated manpower would outrun the demand for it and that, even where employed, educated manpower would find the jobs available unsatisfying. While only about 20% of the jobs in the 1970s will require post high-school education, according to a Bureau of Labor Statistics' study they cite, about one-half of the college age cohort will have gone to college, at least for some period. In short, and as their study argues, almost half of that cohort may find itself underemployed, working at jobs requiring less education than they have, and less interesting than they had sought. "Nearly 30 per cent of four year male college graduates are [even] now in blue-collar, sales, and clerical jobs . . . which do not make full use of their education." If this continues unchecked, states the Carnegie Commission report, ". . . we could end up . . . with a political crisis . . . as in Ceylon or in India or in Egypt."

According to a special task force of the Department of Health, Education and Welfare (in 1972), there is ". . . growing disgruntlement of white-collar workers and the growing discontent among managers." Various studies have thus found increased job-turnover in white-collar jobs, increased signs of interest in white-collar unions, increased reluctance of students to accept closely supervised jobs, a considerable decline among students in their belief in the rewards of hard work, a declining sense of loyalty to employers among white-collar workers, and an increased interest of middle managers in joining a union.[90]

In the Spring 1977 *Occupational Outlook*, Russell B. Flanders, a division head of the U.S. Bureau of Labor Statistics, noted that the U.S. "labor force rose from an average of 10.9 years in school in 1952 to 12.5 in 1974. Specifically, the proportion of the labor force completing at least 4 years of college rose from about 8 to 15 per cent during this period." In little more than twenty years, then, the proportion of college graduates has nearly doubled, reaching a point where in 1974 about one in seven members of the labor force had finished college. In particular, the proportion of college graduates among minority groups in the labor force had increased about 400%, climbing to 9.3% in 1974 from 2.6% twenty years earlier. Without doubt, the deteriorating market situation for educated manpower will have a particularly great danger for them.

It is important to note that Flanders concludes that "despite a possible modest decline in college enrollments in the future, the proportion of college graduates in the labor force may reach 20% by 1985 . . . [and] the number of college graduates will probably continue to increase by record numbers each year through the 1970s. The quantity of college degrees awarded is expected to increase by 15 per cent between 1974 and 1985."

Flanders' "supply-demand figures indicate that the number of college graduates entering the labor force over the 1974–85 period would be about 950,000 above the number of job openings projected for college graduates." As a result, a spillover "of college graduates into nontraditional fields has already become apparent. For example, between 1970 and 1974, the proportion of workers having four or more years of college education increased by more than 60 per cent in clerical, service, and blue-collar occupations. . . . Prospects are no brighter for scientists and engineers holding doctoral degrees than they are for college graduates generally."

The Summer 1973 issue of *Occupational Outlook*, discussing the Manpower Report of the President, observes that a "sharp reduction in births since the late 1950s has already led to a decline in enroll-ments at elementary school levels. Enrollments in public and private schools have dropped from a peak 36.8 million in 1969 to an es-timated 35.6 million in 1972 and are expected to fall to 33.3 million in 1977, a net decline of nearly 3.5 million . . . secondary school enroll-ments are expected to decline from a peak of 16.0 million during the mid-1970s to 14.3 million in 1981. . . . Rather than the steadily in-creasing demand for teachers which took place during the past two decades . . . the remaining years of the 1970 decade will witness a drop in the total demand for elementary and secondary school teachers in spite of increasing replacement requirements. . . . Be-tween 1972 and 1976 an average reduction of 13,000 in new teaching jobs will occur . . . and a further reduction in demand will occur, for the same reason, the following five years as well. The result will be a decline in the average annual demand for new teachers from a peak of 214,000 a year between 1967 and 1971 to 182,000 a year between 1972 and 1976 . . . the demand for college teachers [however] will continue to rise during the early 1970s . . . but most of this demand will be for replacements to fill vacancies left by teachers who retire or leave the profession for other reasons. After 1976, the average annual increase in demand for college teachers will decline to 14,000 a year from 26,000 a year between 1967 and 1971."

In the Winter 1975 *Occupational Outlook*, Elinor W. Abramson, labor economist with the U.S. Bureau of Labor Statistics, reports that ". . . job openings for doctoral degree workers between 1972 and 1985 would total about 187,000. The available supply during the same period, however, is estimated at about 580,000 persons. Therefore, if present trends continue in patterns of use of Ph.D.s relative to other workers and in the proportion of persons obtaining doctoral degrees, by 1985 more than twice as many Ph.D.s would be available for work in Ph.D.-type jobs as there are jobs . . . in physics, the supply would be about half again more than the demand; in mathematics, only about one-eighth more. In contrast, projected supply may be twice as high in life science or social science and psychology; 3 times in arts and humanities; 4½ times in education; and 8½ times in busi-ness and commerce."

The market pressure, then, on the New Class promises to grow sharply for the foreseeable future; if it continues, even the usually ad-vantaged technical intelligentsia will feel increasing pressure. As a result of their commonly blocked ascendence, there would be a grow-ing likelihood of increased unity of the New Class in its various and diverse forms and, indeed, of a unity that may well take the form of an increasing radicalization directed against the old class.

If the growing oversupply of educated manpower produces intensified alienation and unity among the New Class, it will not however be the first time that this has happened in the West. Much the same thing had already occurred during the great Depression of the 1930s in England, the United States, France, not to speak of Germany where it sent some of the New Class into the Nazi movement. Indeed, it is precisely because of the Nazi and Fascist experience of the thirties that it cannot be glibly supposed that the alienation of the New Class must necessarily move it toward the left and toward solidarity with the old working class.

*11.19 Addendum on Student Rebellions:*  How may we understand the relationship between the student rebellions of the 1960s and the New Class? Even a first glance suggests important linkages. For one, the rebelling students were themselves trainee members of the New Class. This, however, is *not* to refer vaguely to their "bourgeois origins"—for this conflates the distinction between old and new class—but, rather, to hold more precisely with Richard Flacks that: "Virtually all studies of protesters indicate that the average family income of activists is higher than that characteristic of their non-activist classmates. But the source of this income is special—it derives from occupations that are intellectual or professional in character. Not only are the children of blue-collar and lower white-collar workers underrepresented in the movement, but so are offspring of business executives and entrepreneurs." [91]

The activists were often the children of an older generation of the New Class, often liberal, urban professionals working for large buroorgs, and whose child-rearing practices typically imparted concern for autonomy and a scepticism of traditional authority. These parents commonly taught that authority was not right just because it was authority, that people had to give and be given reasons for their actions and policies, and that these had to be grounded in some set of "principles." In other words: the student rebels in the United States and other western countries had often learned the rudiments of CCD from their parents *long before they went to college.* Indeed, if one looks at the earlier student rebels of the 1960s, there is a clear continuity between their parents' liberal values and their own autonomy-striving; in fact, about one-sixth of the early student rebels, the movement's "yeast," were from left-leaning families and had participated in a family-sustained tradition of political dissidence. [92]

The importance of CCD—family-imparted or otherwise—for political alienation of the student rebels is further suggested by the fact that the rebellion was greatest among students in the humanities, liberal arts, or the theoretical sciences which remain the campus strongholds of the CCD. Correspondingly, the rebellion was also strongest on elite campuses where education does not readily become narrow vocational training, and where the humanities and theoretical sciences remained important.

Was there, then, no connection between economic developments and the student rebellion? I believe there was but not, as is sometimes suggested, because students fearfully anticipated impending unemployment or unsatisfying jobs. I would instead focus on faculty financing during this period, whether financing of their research or of their own salaries which came to be (and still are) linked to their ability to raise outside research funds. One consequence of increased outside funding was that faculty members became more independent and less responsive to internal controls by their college administration. A second was that faculty whose research funds were sharply increased (for example, in the social sciences) and whose salaries consequently improved more than others, were spending more time doing research and had less "contact hours" with students. Teaching was often turned over to hard-working teaching assistants who, along with the increased numbers of research assistants, became a kind of junior proletariat, thrust into the market at a low level of skill and with a high work load. In this respect, the growing numbers of graduate students made possible by increased research-funding were not so different from the junior faculty itself. In short, the academic "proletariat" was burgeoning. Less fortunate faculty in the humanities were unable to keep up with the boom in academic research funding in the social sciences and were thus unable to keep their salaries abreast; they were experiencing a relative deprivation and a growing alienation that might spread to their own students. For these reasons the vanguard of the student protest in the 1960s was in the united forces of the social sciences and the humanities.

Much has been made of the strong correlation between student protest and the size of the campus, protest apparently increasing with increased size. In some part increased size facilitated protest by fostering a bureaucratized, routinized, campus atmosphere having fewer personal ties that might inhibit conflict. Increased campus size would also be particularly resented by students coming from the New Class with an orientation to the culture of critical discourse. For inherent (if implicit) in CCD is a model of *education* involving *responsive* social interaction, an expectation that they were entitled to voice their criticisms, that their "lowly" estate did not disqualify their opinions, and did not entitle authority to leave them unnoticed and unanswered. With the increasing size of classes and the increasing isolation of elite professors absorbed in well-funded research, the model of education implicit in CCD was increasingly violated. As the selves (or egos) of the lowly are acknowledged by the CCD, since even *their* beliefs are in principle entitled to as much of a hearing as those higher and older, *the young and lowly have a vested interest in CCD.* With the violation of the culture of CCD, by reason of larger, more regimented schools, there was also a demeaning of self suffered by students, particularly those early trained in CCD. This injury to self was linked to the denial of full adulthood typically experienced by those living through the role "moratorium" as students. The decline of discourse was thus experienced as part of the denial of full adult participation, and as a further blockage of the student's ascendence to adulthood.

This is not to say that the larger campuses had no other effect on student protest. Larger classes meant an increasing "span-of-control," the average faculty member had to control more students; declining student-faculty contact hours and the increased use of student assistants instead of professors for teaching, meant the waning effectiveness of university authority. This occurred not only on campus and in classrooms, but also in residence halls and student housing, where university authority broke down almost entirely with burgeoning enrollments. Moreover, as campus housing could not keep up with student expansion, students were increasingly housed off-campus in student ghettos, remote from university controls. Thus increased size meant increased student alienation and the thinning out and even breakdown of the university control over students. The same factor that intensified student alienation thus also impaired the ability of university authorities to contain it.

In general, however, too much has been made of the schools' increasing size in explaining the student revolt of the 1960s, largely because current analyses are typically lacking in historical perspective and cross-national data. Student movements and "revolts" are surely not new: there was the Russian student revolutionary and Narodnik movement of the 1860s and 1870s, the German student movement in the first quarter of the nineteenth century associated with Germany's emerging nationalism, the Chinese student movement emerging after the Russian Revolution, the Parisian student movement of the 1830s, and many others. In none of these early revolts was there *mass* education, and the university was then far from "industrialized." Size, then, when viewed in an historical and comparative perspective, is not a necessary condition for the alienation of students.

# Thesis Twelve: The Family in the Reproduction of Alienation

12.1 How does alienation get sustained through time and how is it reproduced? The most fundamental mechanism for that reproduction is social *organization*. Alienation must in some ways find a protective group setting if it is to be sustained and passed on. There are at least two basic forms for the group reproduction of alienation, one, very ancient, nothing less than the family itself; the other, very modern, the "vanguard" organization.

12.2 To sustain alienation, persons need the support and protection of others—family, friends, comrades. When political deviance is implanted in some form of boundaried group organization, a new and major stage in the alienation of the New Class has been reached. Such groups can be formed in many different conditions and around different activities. Group solidarity can, for example, develop among the members of the editorial committee of some dissident journal or newspaper. For a period, the heart of the old Bolshevik Party was the editorial committee of its newspaper, *Iskra*, and the Party itself was at first fundamentally conceived as the instrument of these editors. Again, men in prison or in exile may become close to one another and form loose groupings for mutual protection.

12.3 But there is one group—the family—that already exists. It does not need to be created, it can be captured. Before the political organization with its protective comrades, the family is often the first group won by the politically alienated person. Often the family is the first "public" of the alienated youth, the captive audience, whom he attempts to win over. At the lowest level, the family may help simply by not turning the deviant in and by concealing his dissidence from authorities. Some families, fearful of "trouble," will indeed turn the dissident in; others may risk everything to hide him when he is "on the run." This is the primitive germ material, the elemental stuff, of which guerilla warfare is a lineal if distant connection.

It would be provincial to assume, however, that family alienation begins only with alienation of the children. In colonial situations, for example, a father may go over to the nationalist cause, bringing his family with him. Here the family is alienated from the "top down."

A decisive moment in the alienation of a family occurs when the father, or another member of the family is injured, jailed, or executed because of his political activities: e.g., Lenin's brother. This often unites the family, crystallizing its alienation, sharpening its solidarity against the public authorities; modern public politics then becomes subtly and invisibly interwoven with the ancient family feud.

The family can also become the primitive political "cell," socializing the young in the family's rebel political tradition. Here the family may serve to protect and to transmit, even across generations, a radical tradition. It transforms a personal radicalism into a family tradition. Kenneth Keniston, for example, has noticed that many of the young radicals of "the new left" of the 1960s were the children of "old left families." Richard Cobb has also noticed the family transmission of the French revolutionary tradition following 1789.

Where a family has been bloodied in struggle against a colonial imperialism or internal despotism, rebellion may then become a family project: one generation has invested its blood, the widows never let the young forget the sacrifice, and finally, "the sons of the widows" may reap the revolution.

*12.4 An Argument:* Yes, *most often* the family serves as a transmission belt for traditional values, *discouraging* its members from political and other deviance. Indeed, most other institutions support the *status quo* most of the time. Our aim, however, is *not* to understand what happens most of the time, but how that extraordinary event, rebellion against tradition and the *status quo,* is possible. If families were solidary in ostracising political deviants there would probably be less of it; conversely, a surprising amount of political deviance is supported by that supposed pillar of the *status quo,* the family. In many societies, family loyalties are such that members have a claim on kin support even against the rest of society. The same cannot be said of most other institutions to which people belong. The very structure of the family makes it vulnerable to the claims of political dissidents.

# Thesis Thirteen: Dilemmas of Marxism and the Vanguard Organization

13.1  To understand the vanguard organization and its role in the protection of intellectuals' political alienation, it is helpful to understand Marxism and its own contradictions: Marxism has always lived a double life, vaunting theory, arguing that emancipation from the present cannot be achieved without it, yet suspecting and sneering at theorists. Theory is seen as necessary to escape from the pull of the encompassing bourgeois culture; but the theorist is seen as grounded in the old, comfortable bourgeoisie or in the timid, loquacious university academics, who will presumably "go over" only in the last hours of the battle. Marxism wishes to vaunt the function, but to stigmatize the functionary. This serves to conceal the alien *elite* origins of its own theory, so dissonant in a social movement purporting to be proletarian. That is why Marxism aims at the "unity of theory and praxis" saying nothing about its relationship to the theory-*maker*, to the theorist-intellectual. [93]

Marxism's stress on the role of theory and of "scientific" socialism must inevitably invest theorists, intellectuals—in a word, the New Class—with great authority. For it is they and they alone who produce socialism's theory. But how can the proletariat submit itself to the tutelage of theory without also submitting to the invisible pedagogy of *intellectuals*—the New Class? Marxism's task is to find a way of vaunting theory but concealing the New Class from which it derives, concealing its paradoxical authority in a movement of proletarians and socialists. The invention of the vanguard party was central in that maneuver.

13.2  Marxism is the false consciousness of cultural bourgeoisie who have been radicalized. "When the (First) International was formed," wrote Marx, "we expressly formulated the battle cry: The emancipation of the working class must be conquered by the working classes themselves." But who was the "we" who formulated that battle cry?

Commitment to the *self*-emancipation of the proletariat is an act of theory made by a theoretical elite and therefore embodies a profound false consciousness.

In holding that the working class will set *itself* free, there are two elements of false consciousness: (1) that the class *to be set free* is the working class, whereas in fact it is the cultural bourgeoisie; (2) that the class *to make that emancipatory act* will be the working class, whereas they will succeed in doing this only under the political leadership and cultural tutelage of the cultural bourgeoisie.

13.3   Marxism itself was made, after all, by the son of a minor Prussian bureaucrat and the son of a multi-national industrialist, both of mandarin culture.

Marxism has always been suspicious of the native culture of the proletariat—for their lack of a CCD.[94] When Lenin encoded the Vanguard Organization, one of its central objectives was to protect the purity of the *teoretiki from the working class*. Lenin, following Kautsky, unblinkingly understood that Marxism was the creation of educated intellectuals. He held that socialism could not be spontaneously created by the proletariat and had, instead, to be brought to it from the outside, which was the mission of the Vanguard Party. The vanguard was to maintain a strict hierarchical structure, "democratic centralism," in order to ensure that the party remained under the firm control of those possessing CCD or "scientific" theory, the *teoretiki*, making the party the imprinting mechanism of the intellectuals.

13.4   While Marxism regarded theory as indispensable for revolutionary emancipation, it believed that theory could come neither from the workers themselves nor from ordinary middle class academicians. How then could the necessary theory be developed? Plainly, a special type of theorist was needed. And if a special theorist was needed a special organization was also needed to develop, protect, fine-tune and empower him. This was the Vanguard Organization. It was the latent function of the Vanguard Organization to overcome—partly to paper-over and partly genuinely to transcend—the contradiction between Marxism's insistence on theory and its distrust of theorists.

13.5   Make no mistake about it, the Marxist critique of theorists reveals a real dilemma of any social theory that aims to speak truly, *correctly* noting its vulnerability to the *status quo,* and *validly* observing its corruptibility. This is especially true of theory that sets out to transcend the present, but it is no less true of "normal" academic social theory. Unlike academic social theory, however, which has the false consciousness that it is "value free," Marxism correctly understood that a theory's very *social* involvement exerts an unremitting pressure on it. It therefore sought to establish the *organizational* requirements of an emancipated and emancipating social theory. This is a problem which academic social theory has never even begun to address, for it *assumes* that the university already has created its own organizational requirements. Neither theory is what it believes itself to be. Academic social theory is not value free, and Marxism is not the consciousness of the proletariat. Both reflect the consciousness of the New Class whose will to power takes different paths.

13.6 Marxism's solution to the organizational requirements of theory was the invention of the Vanguard Party, which was originally encoded by Lenin in his world-shaping book, *What Is to Be Done?* The Vanguard Organization mediates between the New Class and the working class (peasantry or proletariat). On the one side, it is the instrument with which the radicalized segment of the New Class politically mobilizes and re-educates the working class. On the other, the Vanguard Organization is an instrument through which this part of the New Class protects itself from its enemies *and from its working class allies,* insulating the fighting elite of the New Class from tendencies to accommodation (opportunism) and from tendencies toward an isolating ideological purism (sectarianism).

13.7 The Vanguard Party, however, is not just a transmission belt; it is not just the organizational expression of a consciousness and ideology that alienated intellectuals had developed before entering the Party. Even though the Vanguard's central cadres are first derived from intellectuals, the Vanguard is not just a disguise and "front group" for them. If the Vanguard is an instrument of sections of the New Class intellectuals, it is also an instrument for their *transformation*. Some of this transformation of the New Class is a "radicalization" brought about by deepening their involvement in struggle against the system in power. This is a form of radicalization, born not of economic deprivation but of *political* suffering. It is radicalization by way of the agonic strife of an elite: "heroic" suffering.

The Vanguard moves parts of the New Class from alienation to radicalization. Alienation precedes the New Class's involvement with the Vanguard; it is later cumulatively committed in the course of intensifying political struggles. As a result of these cumulative commitments it is increasingly difficult for parts of the New Class to find their way back into normal careers or to live conventional family lives. Their future, therefore, is tied increasingly to the struggle against the *status quo*. It is an important function of the Vanguard to provide solidarities enabling the radicalized sector of the New Class to cope with anxieties aroused by their dangerous confrontation with established authority and by their isolation from normal careers and family life.

There is a feed-back cycle here: the Vanguard Organization exacerbates the radicalized New Class's anxieties, by reason of its confrontations with authority and then teaches the New Class to control these anxieties by doing *political work*. Defining politics as a form of self-and-world transfoming *labor*, a labor of redemption, the Vanguard Party is Protestantism politically radicalized and radicalism ascetically disciplined.

*13.8*   The Vanguard, then, is not just a simple extension of the New Class but an organizational *mediation* of its political practice. It develops its own logic and its own distinct interests that soon conflict with those of the originating intellectuals. As I have said, the common ideology of intellectuals is an ideology about discourse that places a central value on talk; but the military exigencies and dangers of the Vanguard lead it to insist on disciplined obedience. Intellectually this means: discourse and critique must give way to the "line." As encoded by Lenin, the Vanguard is grounded in the *limitation of discourse*. The Vanguard is a *symptom* that expresses ambivalence toward intellectuals: the need for *and* the distrust of them. Who needs *discussion* groups? asked Lenin in disgust. In time, then, intellectuals, who are more useful during the early stage of political mobilization, are superseded by the technical intelligentsia.

But this does not imply an end to the leadership of intellectuals elsewhere, in later revolutions. The success of Fidel Castro's group of militant, university-trained military intellectuals was furthered precisely because they had positioned themselves outside of the Cuban "vanguard." The Cuban Revolution exhibits how a group of radicalized intellectuals, rather than being the tool of the Communist Party, transformed it into their own instrument, at least for a while. Whoever ultimately inherits the Cuban Revolution, there is little doubt that it was at first led by intellectuals.

*13.9*   A key function of the Vanguard is to generate a system of control over intellectuals. This was clearly Lenin's intent in his debate with Martov and others at the 1903 Congress of their party where they insisted that intellectuals, like others, had to accept party discipline if they wanted to be members. Without the Vanguard, the only controls to which the intelligentsia are subject are those of their professions, universities, and the culture-markets. The Vanguard, then, is *a* solution to the problem of extricating intellectuals from the control of respectable institutions and bourgeois culture.

But the Vanguard does not actually subject intellectuals to the control of the *proletariat*. Rather, the Vanguard exposes intellectuals to the control of other intellectuals who have been resocialized as a party cadre. The Vanguard's senior intellectuals re-socialize themselves in the very process of re-socializing novice intellectuals.

The Vanguard Party has certain churchly qualities, and C.L.R. James once called them "proletarian Jesuits." As the Jesuits purported to act in the interests of the church, so too, does the proletarian vanguard purport to act in the interests of "its" class. But the proletariat is "its" class only in the way a tribe "belongs" to the anthropologist who studies it and calls them "my people."

*13.10*   The Vanguard itself is actually divided into two elites, a first-class elite and a second-class elite. The first-class elite are the "full-timers," the "professional revolutionaries" of whom Lenin spoke; the second-class elite are the part-timers who spend most of their time earning a living, with which they contribute to the support of the full-timers. The machinery of the Vanguard is always in the hands of the full-time functionaries, who are persons to whom politics comes before the intellectual life. They are intellectuals (or intellectualized) persons who have gone over to full-time politics, and who control the socialization and org-environment of the part-timers. The intellectuals, then, are transformed by their recalcitrant organizational tool.

After the capture of state power, the position of the Vanguard itself becomes precarious. In Russia it was pulverized by Stalinism;[95] and in China by the Cultural Revolutions. If the Vanguard transforms intellectuals for its own interests, the state in turn transforms the Vanguard into its tool.

*13.11*   The control structure of "socialism" is definable in terms of three intercalcating levels: The New Class, Vanguard, and state. Each strives to maintain its relative autonomy vis-à-vis the other two. There is both integration and contradiction among all the levels. The requisites for the autonomy of the New Class are undermined by the Vanguard and the latter's autonomy is subverted by the state. The more that the New Class and Vanguard seek to use the state for their own interests, the less autonomy can they have from the state.

13.12 Given a tightly disciplined Vanguard Organization, there need be no one special set of social conditions necessary for revolution. All that may be further needed is the effective mobilization of such discontent as exists and the exploitation of some calamitous historical episode. Leninist Vanguards, however, have commonly succeeded only in relatively under-developed areas where the moneyed classes were still immature, where land-based elites were discredited and the state weak or disrupted.

13.13 The future of the *Leninist* type of Vanguard, then, is linked to the politics of the *undeveloped* regions. Here they succeed when faced with an undeveloped state apparatus, or where the state's repressive instruments, especially the army, have been crushed by another state. The October Revolution was prepared for by Lenin's Vanguard *and by the German Army* (and not without some arms-length arrangements with one another). It is unlikely, however, that the Leninist Vanguard will have much success with an intact state in an advanced industrial society and with a modern system of mass communication. Vanguard initiatives are most likely to succeed where mass loyalties to the state have been undermined by vast military catastrophes and/or by the humiliating subservience of its own impotent elite to a foreign imperialism.

13.14 In the West, therefore—in Western Europe, the United States and, perhaps, also in Japan—the Leninist type of Vanguard has reached its high water mark and is under pressure to transform itself. The old Leninist Vanguard was initially forged in a period of imminent revolution from 1900–1917 and where vast social catastrophes were plainly imminent since 1905. The old Vanguard only needed to prepare itself for targets of opportunity. The new Vanguard will be more Gramscian, organized for a long war of ideological attrition, seeking slowly to wrest ideological hegemony from the old class well before it makes its bid for power. It holds that "the reformation must come before the revolution." It is the Gramscian Vanguard,[96] prepared for a long "war of position" rather than the Leninist war of maneuver, that is the organizational infra-structure of the emerging Eurocommunism.

*13.15 A Problem:* Is there a contradiction here? That is, if the New Class is characterized by its commitment to CCD, then how can it also join the Vanguard Party which limits and acts inimically toward CCD? This, of course, is only a special case of a more general question: how can anybody belong to any group or organization that impairs their interests? Once we see the general character of the question, we can recognize how very common it is for people to do such things. Why, then, do intellectuals join the Vanguard even though the Vanguard limits the rationality to which they are committed?

*One answer:* intellectuals, like anyone else, are commonly involved in a trade-off, sacrificing some of their values to achieve others. They may well anticipate that their CCD will be circumscribed. In return for this, however, some expect and indeed do receive compensatory increments of solidarity, of group membership, of relief from loneliness and, above all, some receive a sense that through their membership they may personally overcome their sense of powerlessness and, as the expression has it, place their hand on "the wheel of history."

The fundamental, underlying structure is this: intellectuals, like others, seek to equilibrate power and goodness. They want power commensurate with what they think to be their own value, and intellectuals have a very high opinion of their value. Having power, increasing their power, is therefore very important to some of them. This is an aspect of the Platonic Complex, but in its basic structure is not peculiar to the New Class.

*Second answer:* as I have said repeatedly, the New Class (like other groups) is a *contradictory* class. Certain of its interests, particularly its interest in CCD, dispose it toward freedom. But its other interests, as a cultural bourgeoisie, make it an elite concerned to monopolize incomes and privileges. What is involved is a trade-off in which some interests are sacrificed for others.

Many intellectuals, however, do *not* believe that there *is* any sacrifice at all in joining the Vanguard. They may simply not believe that the Vanguard is truly opposed to freedom and, especially, freedom of discussion. When still outside the Vanguard Party they may regard such claims as the prejudices of the bourgeoisie and of its communication media. Once having joined the Vanguard, however, many think otherwise. Clearly, this has been the case for thousands of intellectuals throughout the world who have produced a vast literature of disillusionment about "the god that failed." There is no doubt that intellectuals have been central to the design of the Vanguard; there is no doubt that intellectuals have been central to the revolution-making process and to the politburo and leading committees of the Vanguard; there is also no doubt that thousands of intellectuals have joined the Vanguard and, then, *quit it in disgust.*

13.16   Since intellectuals of the New Class commonly oppose censorship, it comes as no surprise that the New Class in the Soviet bloc has been one of the centers of resistance to the Soviet regime.[97] We need to remember, however, that the censorship so disturbing to the New Class manifests itself well before "socialism" captures state power.

Vanguard parties, conceived on Lenin's model, were from the beginning designed to *control* intellectuals and to *limit* the culture of critical discourse. A central organizational principle of the Vanguard party, "democratic centralism," limits the time within which discussion can exist and insists that, after a decision has been made, the discussion ends and is not to be pursued endlessly, that when ended the majority position must be supported publicly even by those members of the group who oppose it. From the beginning, Leninism meant an end to "discussion groups."

The idea of free discussion, although central to the culture of critical discourse, is essentially contradicted by the New Class's own character as a cultural bourgeoisie. As the bearers of the CCD, the New Class opposes censorship, but as a cultural bourgeoisie with its own vested interests, it may wish to limit discussion to members of its own elite: and it may also seek state management of the economy to remove the blockages to its own ascendance, thereby exposing itself to censorship and other controls by the very state they foster.

Eurocommunism is an effort at a mini-max solution to that contradiction. That is, on the one hand, Eurocommunism remains committed to the extension of the state's sway over the economy, thereby removing career blockages for the New Class and, on the other, it renounces the "dictatorship of the proletariat" and commits itself to a pluralistic democracy thus limiting the threat of censorship. For the radicalized sector of the New Class, Eurocommunism is an optimum compromise and is the price that they have demanded increasingly in Western Europe for their support of the Communist Party.

# Thesis Fourteen: The Flawed Universal Class

*14.1* The New Class is the most progressive force in modern society and is a center of whatever human emancipation is possible in the foreseeable future. It has no motives to curtail the forces of production and no wish to develop them solely in terms of their profitability. The New Class possesses the scientific knowledge and technical skills on which the future of modern forces of production depend. At the same time, members of the New Class also manifest increasing sensitivity to the ecological "side effects" or distant diseconomics of continuing technical development. The New Class, further, is a center of opposition to almost all forms of censorship, thus embodying a universal societal interest in a kind of rationality broader than that invested in technology. Although the New Class is at the center of nationalist movements throughout the world, after that phase is secured, the New Class is also the most internationalist and most universalist of all social strata; it is the most cosmopolitan of all elites. Its control over ordinary "foreign" languages, as well as of technical sociolects, enable it to communicate with other nationalities and it is often a member of a technical guild of international scope.

*14.2* For all that, however, the New Class is hardly the end of domination. While its ultimate significance is the end of the old moneyed class's domination, the New Class is also the nucleus of a *new* hierarchy and the elite of a new form of cultural capital.

The historical limits of the New Class are inherent in both the nature of its own characteristic rationality, and in its ambitions as a cultural bourgeoisie. Its culture of critical discourse fosters a purely "theoretical" attitude toward the world. Speakers are held competent to the degree that they know and can *say* the rules, rather than just happening to follow them. The culture of critical discourse thus values the very theoreticity that the "common sense" long suspected was characteristic of intellectuals.

Intellectuals have long believed that those who know the rule, who know the theory by which they act, are superior because they lead an "examined" life. They thus exalt theory over practice, and are concerned less with the success of a practice than that the practice should have submitted itself to a reasonable rule. Since intellectuals and intelligentsia are concerned with doing things in the right way and for the right reason—in other words, since they value doctrinal conformity for its own sake—they (we) have a native tendency toward ritualism and *sectarianism*.

14.3   The culture of the New Class exacts still other costs: since its discourse emphasizes the importance of carefully edited speech, this has the vices of its virtues: in its *virtuous* aspect, self-editing implies a commendable circumspection, carefulness, self-discipline and "seriousness." In its negative modality, however, self-editing also disposes toward an unhealthy self-consciousness, toward stilted convoluted speech, an inhibition of play, imagination and passion, and continual pressure for expressive discipline. The new rationality thus becomes the source of a new alienation.

Calling for watchfulness and self-discipline, CCD is productive of intellectual reflexivity *and* the loss of warmth and spontaneity. Moreover, that very reflexivity stresses the importance of adjusting action to some pattern of propriety. There is, therefore, a structured inflexibility when facing changing situations; there is a certain disregard of the differences in situations, and an insistence on hewing to the required rule.

This inflexibility and insensitivity to the force of differing contexts, this inclination to impose one set of rules on different cases also goes by the ancient name of "dogmatism." Set in the context of human relationships, the vulnerability of the New Class to dogmatism along with its very *task*-centeredness, imply a certain insensitivity to *persons*, to their feelings and reactions, and open the way to the disruption of human solidarity. Political brutality, then, finds a grounding in the culture of critical discourse; the new rationality may paradoxically allow a new darkness at noon.

14.4   The paradox of the New Class is that it is both emancipatory *and* elitist. It subverts all establishments, social limits, and privileges, including its own. The New Class bears a culture of critical and careful discourse which is an historically emancipatory rationality. The new discourse (CCD) is the grounding for a critique of established forms of domination and provides an escape from tradition, but it also bears the seeds of a new domination. Its discourse is a lumbering machinery of argumentation that can wither imagination, discourage play, and curb expressivity. The culture of discourse of the New Class seeks to *control* everything, its topic and itself, believing that such domination is the only road to truth. The New Class begins by monopolizing truth and by making itself its guardian. It thereby makes even the claims of the old class dependent on it. The New Class sets itself above others, holding that its speech is better than theirs; that the examined life (*their* examination) is better than the unexamined life which, it says, is sleep and no better than death. Even as it subverts old inequities, the New Class silently inaugurates a new hierarchy of the knowing, the knowledgeable, the reflexive and insightful. Those who talk well, it is held, excel those who talk poorly or not at all. It is now no longer enough simply to be good. Now, one has to explain it. The New Class is the universal class in embryo, but badly flawed.

# Thesis Fifteen: The Political Context

15.1 The political prospect of the New Class depends partly on its own political talents and on the situation within which these must be exercised, not least, the condition of the old class. The first strength of the New Class is its cultural capital. This endows it with bargaining power vis-à-vis the old class, for the latter depends increasingly on the New Class's culture for its own social reproduction.

15.2 Linked to the past by its cultural heritage, the New Class is also *freed* from the past by its CCD. Both its historical rooting and its utopian perspective allow it continuity in time. Its orientation to the "totality" endows it with a cosmopolitanism facilitating political diagnosis, the decoding of events in the largest context, from a national, international, and increasingly, a world-system standpoint. In general, the decoding power of the New Class, being a function of its cultural stock, is unsurpassed by any other class. This means that its capacity for political diagnosis or orientation is also unsurpassed.

15.3 The promise of the New Class is that it itself can (unlike the old class) live by a set of rules because it has no selfish interest leading it systematically to depart from its own rules and from a concern to "serve the people." Yet the New Class also thinks its own culture of critical discourse best, which is to say that it lives a contradiction. On the one side, its CCD presses to undermine all societal distinctions and, on the other, believing its own culture best it wishes to advantage those who most fulfill and embody it. Its own culture, then, contains the New Class's "seeds of its own destruction."

15.4 While the New Class understands itself as the embodiment of rationality and justice, it is also identified with science and modernization and thus with welfare and power. The posture of the New Class conveys that it can solve the fundamental requisites of the universal grammar of societal rationality: *to reunite both power and goodness*. Having access to the full spread of culture, the New Class is capable of both instrumental rationality and of a Jacobin moralism. Moreover, the New Class's orientation to the "totality" allows it to claim that very "nonpartisanship" which is the essence of all political legitimacy.

15.5 The political weaknesses of the New Class, however, also derive from the CCD to which it is committed. The situation-free character of its language variant dulls its sensitivity to the uniqueness of different situations. Its talents for political *tactics*, then, are inferior to its capacity for diagnosis and *strategy*. The New Class's political skills are limited also by its theoreticity, which generally sours it for action and impairs its sensitivity to the feelings and reactions of others.

There is, however, one major ideology of the modern era that does not share these liabilities—Marxism. *With its special accent on "the unity of theory and practice," and on the contextual analysis of historically concrete situations, Marxism is a specific corrective for the political limits built into the ideology of discourse common to the New Class*. If in some respects Marxism goes beyond CCD, in others, it falls short of it. Marxism is critical discourse retained as a sword against the *status quo*, against the old class. Turned outward only, it is a half compliance with the culture of critical discourse. But it strives to elude theoreticity and abstract formalism, and with this has won a third of the world. It has also paid a price for this: the loss of its capacity for *self*-understanding and development. In many parts of the world, Marxism has been the midwife of the New Class, but those she brings into the world may never see themselves in their own mirror.

15.6 The political achievements of the New Class are as much attributable to the failures, defects, and corruption of the *old* class as to its own political virtues. The old classes that were replaced by revolutionary overthrow have been those that were defeated in war, collaborated with foreign imperialism, were associated with the failure of traditional methods of subsistence-getting, had become passive.

The record in colonial and developing regions is plain enough. There the old class was a scandal: intent on lining its pockets from the crisis of its culture, building its Swiss bank accounts while masses starved, they had lost that fundamental conviction without which no elite can long stay in power; namely, that it is their mission *to serve the people*. Without this sweet false consciousness an elite is simply a gang of scoundrels.

15.7 The weakness of the old class is no sudden, new debility. The old moneyed class was, even when a new rising class, certainly not smiled upon by the older aristocracy they were displacing, nor by the new working class they were exploiting in the industrial slums of Lille and Manchester. The intellectuals and intelligentsia of Europe or America have also commonly seen the bourgeois old class as deficient in civic virtues, social conscience, and cultural sensibility. Intellectuals and intelligentsia of both continents have long sneered at the old class as Babbitts, even if the sneer was followed by a quick look around. And Christians who still believed often saw the bourgeoisie as lacking in fellowship and charity. This Christian reaction was one major source of the Romantic contempt for the "philistinism" of the bourgeoisie. The old class, then, has never been greatly beloved; its grip on society has never been matched by a *legitimacy* of equal force; indeed, it was *born* with a "legitimation crisis."

15.8 To make its condition worse, the old class, unlike earlier hegemonic classes in the West, has had to rule in a very indirect way. Slave owners and feudal nobility were trained to defend their privileges weapons-in-hand. The old class of bourgeoisie, however, governing through a system of Indirect Rule, places the control of force and violence in the hands of others. They themselves have neither taste nor time for practice in violence. (In a way, that was always one of their virtues.) This is transferred to a professional military which increasingly becomes a technical intelligentsia and part of the New Class. Once the military begins to understand that victory or defeat depend on more than hardware or tactics, once it sees that military outcomes depend also on "morale," and hence on socio-economic conditions, the military ceases being a narrow technical intelligentsia and slowly begins to adapt CCD to develop doctrines of revolutionary warfare.

15.9   Nor does the old class normally have the time for the development and assimilation of culture; just as they give others control over the instruments of violence, so, too, do they give others responsibility for developing culture. This means, then, that the defence of the old class, either through violence or through ideology, is not in its own hands. In both cases, it is given over to the New Class.

15.10   Any class aspiring to rule must establish its hegemony in society and this means it must have itself defined as a *legitimate authority*. The universal requirement for legitimacy is that the class must be trusted to rule in a *non-partisan* way on behalf of the *collectivity*. Who now trusts the old class as non-partisan and legitimate? The opinion polls do not show that the large corporations in the United States evoke public confidence. The old class has failed to capture the symbols of legitimacy: i.e., science, morality, technology, professionalism. As it explores *détente* with the USSR, and as its multi-national character becomes known, even its nationalist credentials may become suspect.

The principal factor now maintaining the old class's social power is its economic *productivity: consumerism*. Much of what maintains the old class today is neither brute force *nor legitimacy* but, rather, the masses' sheer experience of consumer gratifications and their association of these with the *status quo*. Yet events such as the "Watergate" scandal can have a profoundly unsettling mass effect. Many now seem as ready to believe in the old class's corruptness as in its moral legitimacy, and perhaps more so. Increasing strains on the economies of neo-capitalist societies, due partly to energy and raw material shortages and to inflation, are also likely to reflect themselves in a further deterioration of the social position of the old class.

15.11   While the legitimacy of the old class in the West has been profoundly vitiated, this was, in many countries, never all that strong in the first place. Yet consumerism still continued to privatize and de-politicize existence; people live a day-to-day existence that seems for the moment to compensate for their often "pointless" lives. Thus while the legitimacy of the old class is continually declining there are still few who seem ready to raise their fist against it—if conditions remain normal. In other words: the old class is best described as inert rather than "stable."

# Thesis Sixteen: Consolations for a Dying Class

We need to remember the world context: the Communist Parties of Italy and France have mass followings and their Eurocommunism remains within arm's-length of government participation, if not of power. The left in Japan is also powerful and militant. Despite the recent oil-borne upturn in England, its old class has long been dying of inflation and taxation at a rapid rate. The idea that the old class has stabilized its condition is an American illusion. Seen from a world standpoint, seen in historical perspective, it becomes clear that the old class has been dying—and with astonishing speed.

16.1   The old moneyed class *is* dying. It is being squeezed out both in slow evolutionary extrusions and in climactic revolutionary explosions. Look at the map in *1916*. The old class was fighting World War I, among other reasons, to establish who controlled the "backward" continents. There was no winner because the old class was smashed in Russia even before it had a chance to come to power. The old class there was eliminated in the name of peace, bread, land, in the name of socialism and human emancipation, in the name of the dictatorship of the proletariat; and then the New Class began its rapid growth.

Look at the map *now*. The feeding-ground of the old class has been pushed back. A new social system has been established in a huge land block ranging from Berlin to Vladivostok and the Eastern islands of China. While the New Class does not govern this land mass, which includes one out of every three persons on earth, still, its power grows continually and will grow still further with the liquidation of

Maoism. And the old class is firmly excluded from the territory. All this, within the space of less than sixty years.

16.2   The United States is the last hope of the old class throughout the world. It is the center of the worldwide forces of the old class today as Sparta was the anchor of the waning aristocracy of ancient Greece. From all over the world, old class money comes streaming into the United States, buying up wheat lands in Kansas and forests in Oregon. The branches of foreign banks proliferate yearly in New York City, being that near-bankrupt city's only growing industry. The international elite of the old class knows what is happening to it; the American sector of the old class, momentarily profiting from the worldwide eclipse of its class, experiences a temporary euphoria from that very world decline.

16.3   The old class in the United States is without doubt the most powerful old class in the world; yet it is dying. *Minor documentation:* "Distrust of government was increasing even before Watergate confirmed the point. The percentage of people who claimed that they did not trust the government 'to do what is right' increased from 22 per cent in 1964, to 37 per cent in 1968, to 76 per cent in 1972. Agreement with the statement that 'the government is run for the benefit of a few big interests' grew from 31 per cent in 1964, to 44 per cent in 1968, to 58 per cent in 1972." [98]

16.4   As the old class stumbles into the future, the production of the New Class grows. Some of the statistics for higher education are relevant: in 1947 (even after the influx of veterans from World War II) there were only some 2.2 million college students in the United States, and they constituted only some 16% of those of college age. From 1955 to 1960, this number increased from 2.6 million to 3.6 million, about 35% of the college age youth. In the 1970s there were some 8 million college students, who were about 40% of the college age youth. By some projections, this is expected to rise to 13 million by the 1980s. Moreover, of those presently in college, some 1,000,000 are graduate students, about 12% of the total. The secular trend of the proportion of college students to those of college age has also been rising since the end of World War II until the present time. In 1947 the bill for higher education was about one billion dollars, in the early 1970s it was about 25 billion dollars, and it is expected to rise to about 44 billion in the 1980s. The New Class is reproducing itself faster than any other class in society.

*16.5* The dying are entitled to a word of consolation: the old class should know, then, that its enemies—or those whom it once thought to be its chief enemies—the "communist" societies of Eastern Europe, are also facing the same destiny. They, too, confront a rising New Class of intellectuals and intelligentsia. Indeed, it may be that the conflict in the East between the old and new classes is even more advanced than it is in the West. For in East Europe, party officials and bureaucrats are even more of an obstacle to New Class technical ambitions than the old class of propertied capitalists in the West. In the East, this conflict has already reached crisis proportions bringing the most repressive measures, including the massive use of arms and armies as in Czechoslovakia. The *intelligenty* of Russia may once again become a distinct and dissident group. The party bureaucrats confine them in concentration camps, throw them into insane asylums where they are drugged into vegetative submission, fire them from their jobs, cast them into exile, and deprive them of citizenship. The ultimate expression, thus far, of the contest between the *intelligenty* and the party officials, however, occurred when the Russians sent tank brigades into Czechoslovakia, to put down the Czechoslovakian "spring" that was largely inspired by the plans of the intelligentsia. East and West, the class in power faces a common challenger.

*16.6* The political basis of *détente* in the USSR is the alliance between the centrist faction of the CPSU (recently headed by Brezhnev) and the Soviet New Class. The Stalinist faction has always suspected the New Class and the New Class has always been its enemy. Internally, the centrist faction today is aimed against the restoration of Stalinism and against the "hards" (recently led by Suslov). The problems of the Soviet economy can be resolved, say the hards, only by a return to Stalinist discipline, austerity, and coercion. The centrists, however, believe that the limits cannot be lifted without ramrodding through a great growth in Soviet productivity. But Soviet resources have repeatedly failed to produce this, so the chiefs of the political center look to the force-feeding of Soviet industry through the intensification of hardware imports from the West, especially the United States. To accomplish this, however, the USSR and Eastern Europe have in a brief time contracted a phenomenal debt.[99]

As distinct from the centrist leaders of the CPSU, the Soviet New Class with whom they are allied supports *détente* as a way of force-feeding industrialization and thereby meeting the growth directives imposed on them and upon which their careers depend. *Détente* also provides occasions for travel to the West by the New Class and for access to cultural stimulation and luxury goods, which are much sought after by them. What the New Class in the USSR wants is plainly foreshadowed in the increasing weekend jaunts by the Yugoslavian New Class to Greece where they take in the sights and stock up on luxuries and on blue jeans, which have become the international uniform of the New Class. In Eastern Europe, *détente* is in part a sop that the center of the CPSU throws to the New Class to prevent it from going the way of the Czechoslovakian Spring. *Détente* and its "fringe benefits" are a way the New Class in the USSR is coopted by the centrist faction of the Communist Party.[100]

16.7   From the American side, *détente* was grounded in the split within the Republican Party. This split was made public at its 1976 convention, where the most politically backward and less educated sections of the old class rallied to the standard of Ronald Reagan. His appeal was most especially to die-hard, anti-communist small businessmen, farmers, ranchers, who are most hostile to the "long hairs" and "theorists" of the New Class. Gerald Ford's victory against Reagan spelled the final defeat of Cold War Communism in the Republican Party by those sectors of the old class in large-scale late-capitalism most allied with the New Class, as well as by many in the New Class itself.

East and West, *détente* is a project of the New Class. In both areas, this is carried out in ways that will for a while maintain the hegemony of the old class in the West and of the Communist Party in the East. At the same time, the trade implications of *détente* can only result in a worldwide intensification of technological development and competition. In the long run, *détente* means the further rise of the New Class and the further decline of the old.

# EPILOGUE

The dying are entitled to a moment of insight and self-recognition. The old moneyed class in the West may discover that its deepest historical affinity with the political elite in the East is that both were transitional classes. In the East, the Vanguard Party was the communist equivalent of the Protestant Reformation; once having paved the way for the New Class, it (like Protestantism) becomes a hollow ideological shell.

The *Communist Manifesto* had held that the history of all hitherto existing society was the history of class struggles: freeman and slave, patrician and plebian, lord and serf, guildmaster and journeyman, and, then, bourgeoisie and proletariat. In this series, however, there was one unspoken regularity: the slaves did not succeed the masters, the plebians did not vanquish the patricians, the serfs did not overthrow the lords, and the journeymen did not triumph over the guildmasters. *The lowliest class never came to power.* Nor does it seem likely to now.

# BIBLIOGRAPHIC NOTE

The theses discussed develop out of a long-established intellectual tradition to which, I hope, they contribute. While the term "New Class" may have first been used by Mikhail Bakunin, he himself was actually only born about the time that the *substantive ideas* with which I am concerned here were first enunciated by the great "utopian" socialist Henri Saint-Simon and his followers. Close on the heels of the revolution of 1789, Saint-Simon prophesied that in the future society administrative authority would no longer be based on coercion, force, or hereditary privilege, but would rely increasingly on possession of expert skills grounded in "positive" knowledge. Saint-Simon, however, did not clearly distinguish between moneyed capital and so-called "human" capital, essentially conflating the two in his notion of a singular vanguard of *industriels*.

His followers (such as Enfantin and Bazard) moved toward socialism because they believed that private property in the means of production meant that this societal resource might be inherited by incompetents who could waste it rather than being controlled by the knowledgeable. It is these early socialists, whom Karl Marx later patronizes as "utopian socialists," because their socialism developed before the full maturation of the proletariat who might enact it. It may be, however, that Marx is best thought of as the last of the utopian socialists (rather than the first of the scientific socialists), for he himself worked before the full maturation of the New Class which his socialism latently represents. I discuss this contention fully in a forthcoming book, *The Two Marxisms.* For bibliographic materials on Saint-Simon and Simonianism, see Emile Durkheim, *Socialism and Saint-Simon (Le Socialisme)* (Yellow Springs, Ohio, 1958), edited by Alvin W. Gouldner, particularly pp. xxviii–xxix, of my introduction.

The tension between property and knowledge, first clearly thematicized by the Saint-Simonians, was later developed in Thorstein Veblen's discussion of the rift between "business" and "industry," between the "captains of industry" controlled by profit motives, and the technologists and engineers who, Veblen complained, were used "only insofar as they would serve . . . commercial profit. . . . To do their work as it should be done these . . . engineers and managers must have a free hand, unhampered by commercial considerations and reservations . . ." (Thorstein Veblen, *Engineers and the Price System* [New York, 1932]). The recent work of Galbraith on the importance of the techno-structure and of Bell on knowledge society are both in the Veblenian tradition, although each minimizes the tensions between knowledge and property that Veblen had highlighted. See, for example, Daniel Bell, *The Coming of Post-Industrial Society* (New York, 1973); and John K. Galbraith, *The New Industrial State* (Boston, 1967) in which the latter argues that "power has, in fact, passed to . . . the association of men of diverse technical knowledge, experience or other talent which modern industrial technology and planning require" (pp. 58–59). It is they, Galbraith holds, not management, who are "the guiding intelligence—the brain—of the enterprise" (p. 71). Bell, for his part, stresses the vast expansion of the technical intelligentsia, observing that its growth rate is two to three times that of the labor force as a whole, and the growing importance of theoretical knowledge for the direction of modern society.

Bell sees the New Class as made up of four "estates," the scientific, technological, administrative, and cultural; while bound by a common ethos, these lack a common intrinsic interest except for learning. It is an open question for Bell whether the New Class can become a single coherent class in society, and, on *this* question, I share his non-doctrinaire open-endedness. For my part, I have in these theses attempted to clarify *the conditions under which the New Class would be more or less alienated from older elites and established institutions, and thus unified, rather than simply to assert the inevitability of that alienation, or of such a unification.*

Midway between Veblen and Bell/Galbraith there was, of course, the classic work of Adolph A. Berle, Jr., and Gardner C. Means, *The Modern Corporation and Private Property* (New York, 1932), and Berle's subsequent, *Power Without Property* (New York, 1959). Berle and Means held that most of the top 200 corporations were management, not owner, controlled. R. A. Gordon subsequently reinforced this with a study that maintained that "the great majority of stockholders have been deprived of control of their property through the diffusion of ownership and growth of the power of management" (R. A. Gordon, *Business Leadership in the Large Corporations* [Berkeley, 1966] p. 250). Maurice Zeitlin's critique of this scholarly tradition is important and we cite and discuss it.

James Burnham's contribution to the intellectual tradition is largely his insistence on the *common* managerial and administrative character of late capitalism *and* Soviet state socialism, thus arguing a version of the convergence hypothesis for modern industrial society akin to that formulated earlier by Max Weber's theory of bureaucracy. (Weber had declared that "it was not the dictatorship of the proletariat but that of the official which was on the march.") See James W. Burnham, *The Managerial Revolution* (New York, 1941). In effect, this study was Burnham's farewell to his earlier Trotskyism which continued to insist that the USSR was a workers' state and still essentially different from a capitalist society, even if now "degenerated." It is crucial to the argument I present, however, that the New Class *not* be reduced to bureaucracy, even though complexly interwoven with and socially close to them.

George Orwell has written a glinting review of "James Burnham and the Managerial Revolution" in which he makes the following penetrating comments: "If one examines the people who, having some idea of what the Russian régime is like, are strongly russophile, one finds that, on the whole, they belong to the 'managerial' class of which Burnham writes. That is, they are not managers in the narrow sense, but scientists, technicians, teachers, journalists, broadcasters, bureaucrats, professional politicians: in general, middling people who feel themselves cramped by a system that is still partly aristocratic, and are hungry for more power and more prestige. These people look toward the U.S.S.R. and see in it, or think they see, a system which eliminates the upper class, keeps the working class in its place, and hands unlimited power to people very similar to themselves. It was only after the Soviet régime became unmistakably totalitarian that English intellectuals, in large numbers, began to show an interest in it. Burnham, although the English russophile intelligentsia would repudiate him, is really voicing their secret wish: the wish to destroy the old, equalitarian version of Socialism and usher in a hierarchical society where the intellectual can at last get his hands on the whip." See George Orwell, *Collected Essays, Journalism and Letters*, vol. 4 (Harmondsworth, 1968).

Weber wrote before the full scientization of the modern bureaucracy and focused on its internal *unity;* I, however, have stressed here and elsewhere the tensions and differences between the linguistic codes used by bureaucrats and by technical intelligentsia (let alone intellectuals). For Weber's position see his "Der Sozialismus," *Gesammelte Aufsätze zur Soziologie und Socialpolitik* (Tübingen, 1924), and his theory of authority of which bureaucracy is only one part, in H. H. Gerth and C. Wright Mills, eds., *From Max Weber: Essays in Sociology* (New York, 1946), especially chapter 8.

Two other important contributions of relevance to the New Class project are Andre Gorz, *Strategy for Labor* (Boston, 1967), and Harry Braverman, *Labor and Monopoly Capitalism* (New York, 1974). Gorz resembles Veblen in his focus on the tension between the "creative" interests of the new working class and the profit-limited conditions under which they work. My own views converge with his when he notes that the new (working) class, interested in its work no less than its income, will press toward self-management. Gorz stresses the contradiction between their control over the productive process and their servitude to the old moneyed class; this is the central mechanism with which he accounts for such New Class alienation as exists. My own accounting for that alienation, however (in Thesis Eleven, et seq.), focuses on five elements of which only one, which I term blockage of technical interests, converges with Gorz's. For other views convergent with Gorz's, see also Serge Mallet, *Essays on the New Working Class* (St. Louis, 1975).

Braverman forcefully argues against the assumption that the labor force has become increasingly skilled and hence that educated labor is now of more strategic importance. He holds that increasing specialization means the destruction of skills, and hence the weakening of their position in the labor market; he contends that the growth of the new class often represents merely a continuation of increasing technical specialization, and thus does not constitute a group different from the "old working class." While it remains an open question as to how far upgraded categories of labor necessarily imply higher skills, still a formal, abstract argument stressing the development of technical specialization does not itself demonstrate that the average skill content of jobs has remained the same or declined; indeed, specialization *can* foster the increase of cumulative knowledge and skills. Some specializations remain static in terms of the skills and knowledge they allow incumbents to acquire, others permit their cumulative development. In any event, Braverman's position is a critique of the assumption that the impact of the New Class would derive from their *functional significance.* Since he holds that there are few workers with significant skills, there are few who are strategically situated to exert effective pressure in pursuit of their own interests and values.

I, for my part, however, do *not* assume that the influence of the New Class (or of any class) derives only from its functional importance, although this *is a* factor. In the contest of classes, the influence of one class is always a function of the growing strength or weakness of others with whom it competes and cannot be assessed out of the total class context. The functional importance of the New Class, then, should not be appraised apart from that of other classes. In appraising the effects of growing specialization on the New Class, one should therefore also appraise the changing functional significance of the *old* moneyed class, and whether it, too, is not undergoing an increased division of labor that also renders its own members ineffectual. The functional significance argument cuts both ways.

What has been happening is the increasing development of the socio-economic system, *qua system,* that is, the increasing mutual dependence of *all* parts on others. There has been a growth of sheer social "systemness." This means that all parts depend increasingly upon others, must increasingly take them into account, and that each has a dwindling power to achieve its ends, so that all may suffer increasing alienation. At the same time, there is a question of the extent to which each class is, *relative to the other*, functionally dependent, and it should not be assumed that all classes depend *equally* on the system in existence. Some, such as the old moneyed class, can not survive the demise of late capitalism; others, such as the New Class, clearly have more functional autonomy and have an historical future apart from it. The New Class can afford to be patient. For my systematic discussion of the notion of functional autonomy/functional dependence, and their relation to power, see A. W. Gouldner, "Reciprocity and Autonomy in Functional Theory," in L. Z. Gross, ed., *Symposium on Sociological Theory* (New York, 1959). Most fundamentally, the influence of the New Class should not be seen as contingent only on its functional significance. Its influence depends *partly* (but only partly) on its functional significance; partly on its possession of the socially specified requisites of privileged office such as education; on its relative functional autonomy; on its political action skills and capacity to mobilize itself and others; on its own numbers and those of its allies; on its will to power; and, very critically, on *the condition of the other classes* with which it competes. Class succession does not come about when one class has defeated another but only when it *replaces* another. The question is who is heir, not simply who is victor. The future of the New Class, then, is not just a question of its technical significance; this is an "economistic" view of class contest. Rather, the future of the New Class also depends greatly on its political skills, which is why I have linked the discussion to the "vanguard" problematic.

One of the most important literatures on the New Class as a world historical phenomenon focuses on its developing role in the Soviet Union. This literature began almost at the start of the Soviet Revolution in the work of Waclaw Machajski (1866–1926) a Polish-born Russian revolutionary plainly influenced by Bakunin's dim view of the New Class, who argued that, for all its proletarian protestations, socialism was the ideology of the rising new middle class of intellectuals and technical intelligentsia. Some of Machajski's writings have been translated and published in V. F. Calverton, *The Making of Society* (New York, 1937). His Polish bibliography may be found in M. Nomad, *Rebels and Renegades* (New York, 1932). My own critique of Machajski may be found in A. W. Gouldner, "Prologue to a Theory of Revolutionary Intellectuals," *Telos*, 26 (Winter 1975–76), especially p. 29 ff. Machajski has had an important influence on the influential political writing of Harold D. Lasswell.

Subsequent discussion of the New Class in the USSR was intensively developed in the works of Leon Trotsky, *Stalinism and Bolshevism* (New York, 1937), and *The Revolution Betrayed* (New York, 1937). Apparently Nicolai Bukharin's own concerns about the New Class in the USSR developed even earlier. See Stephen F. Cohen, *Bukharin and the Bolshevik Revolution* (New York, 1973), p. 142 ff. Cf. Charles Bettleheim, *Les Luttes de Classes en URSS, Deuxième Periode*, 1922–1930 (Paris, 1976). See also Tony Cliff, *State Capitalism in Russia* (London, 1974); M. Yvon, *What Has Become of the Russian Revolution?* (New York, 1937); Peter Meyer, "The Soviet Union, A Class Society" *Politics* (March–April 1944); Adam Kaufman, "Who Are the Rulers in Russia?" *Dissent* (Spring 1954); Milovan Djilas, *The New Class* (New York, 1957). Louis Althusser has argued, with little substantiation, that Stalinism may be understood as a fumbled attack on the New Class. See Louis Althusser, *Essays in Self Criticism* (London, 1976). One of the best studies of the use of higher education in the reproduction of the Soviet intelligentsia is Richard Dobson, "Social Status and Inequality of Access to Higher Education in the USSR," in J. Karabel and A. H. Halsey, eds., *Power and Ideology in Education* (New York, 1977). The most incisive *comparative* analysis of the intelligentsia in the USSR, with that in the late capitalist West, is Frank Parkin's, which concludes that "in socialist society the key antagonisms occurring at the social level are those between the party and state bureaucracy, on the one hand, and the intelligentsia on the other." Parkin shrewdly observes that since the intelligentsia in the West do not confront as sharply defined opponents as they do in the East, they are more likely to accommodate. See Frank

Parkin, "System Contradiction and Political Education," in T. R. Burns and W. Buckley, *Power and Control: Social Structures and Their Transformation* (Beverly Hills, 1976). See also, F. Parkin, *Class Inequality and Political Order* (London, 1971). For a critique of Parkin, see the next article in the Burns and Buckley volume, Russell Hardin, "Stability of Statist Regimes." For analysis of other East European intelligentsia or data on it see also, T. A. Daylis, "The New Economic System: The Role of the Technocrats in the DDR," *Survey* (LXI, 1966); Radovan Richta, *Civilization at the Crossroads: Social and Human Implications of the Scientific and Technological Revolution* (Prague, 1967); Ota Sik, *Plan and Market Under Socialism* (Prague, 1966). Anthony Giddens, *The Class Structure of the Advanced Societies* (London, 1973) has many probing reflections on the East European intelligentsia. Other studies, of many that might be consulted on the Soviet intelligentsia, are Albert Parry, *The New Class Divided* (New York, 1966); G. Churchward, *The Soviet Intelligentsia* (London, 1973); Andras Hegedus, *Socialism and Bureaucracy* (New York, 1976); Serge Mallet, "Bureaucracy and Technocracy in Socialist Countries," *Socialist Revolution* (May–June 1970).

The literature on the New Class and associated issues is of course enormous and cannot be more than briefly mentioned here. In the United States, the important contributions by C. Wright Mills, Edward Shils, S. M. Lipset, Stanley Aronowitz, and David Bazelon are already widely known. An earlier now forgotten study that first interested me in the problem was Lewis Corey, *The Crisis of the Middle Class* (New York, 1935).

The French contribution to this problem has been extremely important. Apart from studies already mentioned, one of the most provocative is Pierre Bourdieu, *Reproduction in Education, Society and Culture* (Beverly Hills, 1977); see also Alain Touraine, *Post Industrial Society* (New York, 1971); and *La conscience ouvrière* (Paris, 1966). Of related interest is the work by Cornelis Castoriardis, *La société bureaucratique* (Paris, 1973) and Claude Lefort, *Eléments d'une critique de la bureaucratic* (Geneva, 1971). These are only among the more recent of a long line of relevant French studies including: Julien Benda, *La trahison des clercs* (Paris, 1927); Louis Bodin, *Les intellectuels* (Paris, 1962); Pierre Naville, *Les intellectuels et la revolution* (Paris, 1927); Paul Nizan, *Les chiens de garde* (Paris, 1932); Pierre Belleville, *Une nouvelle classe ouvrière* (Paris, 1963).

For an extraordinary polemic against intellectuals and, in particular, sociologists, as the exploitative evil genius of the modern period see Helmut Schelsky, *Die Arbeit tun die Anderen: Klassenkampf und Priesterherrschaft der Intellectuellen* (Opladen, 1975). Schelsky is interesting because (unlike Noam Chomsky who thinks intellectuals "evil" and weak) he thinks them evil and *powerful*. (For the fuller implications, see my introduction to this essay.)

Irving Kristol's position is analytically similar to Schelsky's in that he, too, sees the New Class as powerful-and-bad, and particularly so, in its opposition to the "free market" and in its drive toward a planned economy. Thus Kristol holds that the New Class "are the media. They are the educational system," and as a "result of technological, economic, and social developments, this group has become terribly influential." While the New Class has traditionally sought power through persuasion and education, he holds, they now seek to impose themselves "through legislation enabling them to tell people what to do . . ." and are "willing to sacrifice freedom to achieve" their ends. Kristol's position omits discussion of the growing power of the New Class in the *private* sector, ignoring the alienation of large sectors of proprietary ownership by the managerial New Class in the private sector itself. He thus creates the mistaken impression that the New Class is solely a phenomenon of the public sector: "as a group you will find them mainly in the very large and growing public sector. . . ." Nor does Kristol want to confront the fact that the dominant parts of the private sector, the largest corporations, have monopolistic tendencies undermining the very "free market" that, he argues, is subverted by the New Class. Kristol acts as if the growth of state capitalism is taking place behind the back and against the wishes and interests of the private sector; in fact, the private sector itself puts forth all manner of initiatives to have government protect its interests, to subsidize the R & D upon which industry increasingly depends, as well as using the Defense Department as a major market for the private sector. Thus Kristol acts surprised that business has not assumed an aggressive posture toward government and, indeed, does not "even get indignant when some politicians call them bad names." Kristol's defense of the free market system from incursions by the New Class might be more convincing if it were not published in *Exxon, USA* (Third Quarter 1975). *Cf.* Irving Kristol, *Two Cheers for Capitalism* (New York, 1978).

Of my own recent work, the most relevant to this essay is: Alvin W. Gouldner, *The Dialectic of Ideology and Technology* (New York, 1976), and my "Prologue to a Theory of Revolutionary Intellectuals," *Telos* (Winter 1975–76).

# NOTES

1. It is not my intention to suggest that modern intellectuals are merely the secular counterpart of clericals. Indeed, my own stress (as distinct, say, from Edward Shils who does appear to view intellectuals as priests *manqués*) is on the discontinuity of the two.
2. For full development of this, see chapter 2, especially p. 42, of my *Dialectic of Ideology and Technology.*
3. Doubtless some will insist this is a "false consciousness." But this misses the point. My concern here is with their own definitions of their social role, precisely because these influence the manner in which they perform their roles. As W. I. Thomas and Florian Znaniecki long ago (and correctly) insisted, a thing defined as real is real in its consequences. Moreover, the state who employs most of these teachers is itself interested in having teachers consolidate the tie between students and it itself, rather than with the students' parents.
4. See Basil Bernstein, *Class, Codes and Control*, vol. 1, *Theoretical Studies Towards a Sociology of Language* (London, 1971), vol. 2, *Applied Studies Towards a Sociology of Language* (London, 1973), vol. 3, *Towards a Theory of Educational Transmission* (London, 1975). Bernstein's theory is used here in a critical appropriation facilitated by the work of Dell Hymes and William Labov. My own critique of Bernstein emerges, at least tacitly, in the discussion of Thesis Fourteen in the text. It is developed explicitly in my *Dialectic of Ideology and Technology*, pp. 58–66. While Labov has sharply criticized Bernstein, he himself also stresses the general importance of self-monitored speech and of speech *reflexivity* in general (i.e., not only of careful pronunciation) thus converging with Bernstein's focus on reflexivity as characterizing the elaborated linguistic variant and distinguishing it from the restricted variant. See William Labov, *Sociolinguistic Patterns* (Philadelphia, 1972), p. 208.

5. For example: "The Communists disdain to conceal their views and aims. They openly declare . . ." (*Communist Manifesto* [Chicago, 1888], authorized English edition edited by Engels, p. 58).

6. See E. Hobsbawm, *Primitive Rebels* (Manchester, 1959), p. 167 ff.

7. A secret doctrine is one which, because it is reserved only for the organization elite, can be made known only after persons join organizations and reach a certain membership position in it. A secret doctrine thus is never one which can have been a *motive* for joining the organization in the first instance.

8. Lenin's *What Is to Be Done?* was originally published in 1902.

9. I am grounding myself here in the analysis of dimensions of meaning common to social objects in the pioneering work of Charles Osgood and his collaborators. Their researches have recurrently found three dimensions: goodness/badness, weakness/strength, and activity/passivity. In the *Coming Crisis* I proposed an *equilibrium* condition for the first two dimensions, speaking there of social worlds that were culturally permitted and those unpermitted, defining the latter in terms of a dissonance between imputed goodness/badness and weakness/strength. To "normalize" is to contrive to see an unpermitted world as if it were a permitted one, i.e., to remove the dissonance. See A. W. Gouldner, *The Coming Crisis of Western Sociology* (New York, 1970), especially pp. 484–88. For Osgood's first researches see Charles E. Osgood, George Suci, and Percy Tannenbaum, *The Measurement of Meaning* (Urbana, 1957).

10. *The New Industrial State.*

11. *The Coming of Post-Industrial Society.*

12. *The Modern Corporation and Private Property.*

13. "It stands to reason that the one who knows more will dominate the one who knows less," M. Bakouinine, *Oeuvres*, Vol. 5 (Paris, 1911), p. 106.

14. For Machajski's writings, see above, p. 99.

15. Talcott Parsons, *The Social System* (Glencoe, 1951), chapter 10; *Essays in Sociological Theory* (Glencoe, 1954), chapter 18; "The Professions," *International Encyclopedia of Social Sciences* (New York, 1968).

16. While Chomsky's position is exhibited in various of his writings, I shall rely here on his most recent statement in his Huizinga

lecture, "Intellectuals and the State," delivered at Leiden, 9 October 1977. Citations will be from the manuscript copy. Cf. N. Chomsky, *American Power and the New Mandarins* (New York, 1969).

17. Maurice Zeitlin, "Corporate Ownership and Control: The Large Corporations and the Capitalist Class," *American Journal of Sociology* (March 1974), pp. 1073–1119.

18. Obviously, the Manifesto does not reserve the term "class" for those strata characteristic of capitalist society. To ask if the New Class is "really" a class, apart from the question of whether it has certain consequential characteristics in common, is a sterile (not a metaphysical) question. My own position on the question of the *common* characteristics of the New Class is discussed in thesis 6.5.

19. This thesis is developed in Alvin W. Gouldner, "Stalinism: A Study of Internal Colonialism," *Telos* (Winter 1977–78), pp. 5–48. For materials bearing on the thesis that "the peasants, and not the industrial workers, were the main driving force in the [Russian] revolutionary process," see John L. H. Keep, *The Russian Revolution* (New York, 1977).

20. See J. Kelley and H. S. Klein, "Revolution and the Rebirth of Inequality," *American Journal of Sociology* (July 1977). An interesting discussion of the advantages possessed by those with more "human capital" after a revolution, which argues that "if differences in education, skills, language, ability, or other kinds of human capital remain, they will eventually (albeit more slowly) lead to inequality, and unless children are reared apart from their parents, to inherited advantage" (p. 97).

21. The Mexican revolution is often cited as a deviant case, instancing, it is held, a successful revolution in which intellectuals played no leading role. Yet it is appropriate to view the Mexican revolution, with its effort to reform the educational system, to legalize strikes, and redistribute lands (often ambiguously into either private or collective hands) as essentially a *bourgeois* revolution. The local peasant armies that were raised often lacked the kind of integration that ideologizing intellectuals with vanguard organizations can further at the national level. Yet while the Mexican revolution is not the kind of revolution to which our formulation was intended to refer, it is also clear that a very high proportion of intellectuals and intelligentsia joined it. Certainly many of the so-called "precursors" were intellec-

tuals. See James D. Crockcroft, *Intellectual Precursors of the Mexican Revolution* (Austin, 1968). Again, the National Constitutional Assembly of 1916–17 consisted preponderantly of the university educated. If the Mexican revolution is *excluded*, then, it appears that in every major class struggle that eventuated in the capturing of state power *and in a major property transfer in the twentieth century*, the victory was achieved by a political coalition dominated by intellectuals and intelligentsia.

22. Zeitlin, "Corporate Ownership and Control," *American Journal of Sociology* (March 1974), pp. 1073, 1107.

23. Barbara Ehrenreich, "Who Owns America?" *Seven Days* (February 24, 1968), p. 29.

24. See Christopher Lasch, *Haven in a Heartless World: The Family Besieged* (New York, 1977). Lasch clearly shows the growing influence of various "helping" professions over the family but, without the least justification, assumes that this is all fundamentally in the service of capitalism and its *old* class. If so, one wonders why they dislike footing the resultant tax bill?

25. From letter by Cornelis Disco, November 21, 1977.

26. Theses 4.1 and 4.2 are adapted from the Ehrenreich article cited in Table I.

27. Charles Kadushin et al., "Relations Between Elite American Intellectuals and Men of Power," paper presented at the 1973 meetings of the American Sociological Association.

28. Old class domination of the legal control centers of universities and colleges is documented in David N. Smith, *Who Rules the Universities: An Essay in Class Analysis* (New York, 1974). For a summary of various studies of the composition of trustees, see especially chapter 2. There Troy Duster's data shows that the more that trustees think that universities should be run like a business, the less ready they are to allow them academic freedom. However, other data also showed that trustees at private universities are often less disposed to limit academic freedom than those at public universities. As universities and colleges receive increasing funding from governments, the influence of the old class on them weakens. This can occur with the investment of government research for R & D funds in private schools, or through the growth of public schools. Both of these have manifested a long run, secular increase. Thus, expenditures for *private* institutions of higher education grew from $100,300,000 in 1920, to $2,634,000,000 in 1960, and to $31,900,000,000 in

1977. Expenditures for *public* higher education, however, grew from $115,600,000 in 1920 to $3,596,000,000 in 1960 and to $68,100,000,000 in 1977 (*Statistical Abstract of the United States, 1977;* and Fritz Machlup, *The Production and Distribution of Knowledge* [Princeton, 1962], p. 79). Enrollment in private institutions of higher education was 147,000 in 1900 and rose to 1,540,000 in 1960; enrollment in public institutions of higher education was 91,000 in 1900 and 2,210,000 in 1960 (Machlup, ibid., p. 88). Of the total R & D investment in colleges and universities in 1960, $405,000,000 derived from federal funds while only $40,000,000 derived from industry; by 1977 it was estimated that federal R & D funds supplied universities and colleges were $2,634,000,000, while industry supplied $134,000,000 (*Statistical Abstract of the United States, 1977*, p. 612). As the proportion of government funding for universities and colleges increases, university policy increasingly becomes a political question rather than being governed by private trustees. Those controlling schools are then less directly influenceable by the old class, and more directly exposed to public influence and pressure.

29. For amplification see A. W. Gouldner, *The Dialectic of Ideology and Technology*, especially pp. 271–73.

30. Cf. James O'Connor, *Corporations and the State* (New York, 1974), pp. 126–28 for the argument that government financing of R & D and advanced education constitute a socialization of part of the costs of production whose net surplus is privately appropriated.

31. I do not mean to suggest that professionalism is *only* an ideology but only that it is that, *too*. In a welcome effort to demystify the professions (and their study), Eliot Freidson has argued that dedication to service and craftsmanship (which I would *not conflate*) are not distinctive of professionals and "are more usefully treated as elements of an ideology than as empirical characteristics of individual and collective professional behavior. Taken as ideology, they have empirical status as claims about their members made by occupations attempting to gain and maintain professional monopoly and dominance." That ideology may be said to be an important component of the process by which occupations seek to gain and maintain control over their work and working conditions (Eliot Freidson, "The Futures of Professionalisation," in M. Stacey et al., eds., *Health and the Division*

*of Labor* [London, 1977], pp. 32–33). Freidson's work is the productive culmination of the "Chicago Sociology's" long-standing effort to "secularize" the study of occupations and to see professions as just another occupation. For an early effort to distinguish between the Chicago and the Harvard-Columbia approaches to the study of the professions, see A. W. Gouldner, *For Sociology* (Harmondsworth, 1975), p. 17. The Chicago approach minimizes the relevance of skill, craftsmanship, and knowledge, for shaping the work and the guild-political behavior of the professions, tending to suggest that these do not differ consequentially in degree or kind from other occupations. Advanced education is thus here understood not so much as skill- and knowledge-transmitting, but as *legitimations* of privilege and as techniques for allocating jobs and incomes. Skill, knowledge, and education are thus held to be *claimed* by professions as ways of enhancing the privileges and autonomy all occupations are said to want. Two demurrers: (1) That claims to superior skill are so *used*, however, does not demonstrate that such superior skills do not exist. (2) Since all occupations seek autonomy, why is it some win considerably more of it than others? The nature of their skill and knowledge is *one* factor. Granted that the autonomy won does not depend *only* on the special skills of those seeking it, still, valued skills also constitute important groundings of public power and influence. The ideological dimension of professional claims needs to be insisted upon; but this should not exclude recognition of the special skill and knowledge base of some occupations. I would thus distinguish between an occupation's skills and knowledge, on the one hand, and its ideologizing *claims* to skill and knowledge, on the other, and the different *functions* each of these performs. I would distinguish also between claims to skill/knowledge and claims to dedication to the collective weal and would note that the absence of the latter does not *perforce* demonstrate a lack of the former. For other relevant materials see Eliot Freidson, *Doctoring Together* (New York, 1975), and E. Freidson, *Professional Dominance* (New York, 1970); E. C. Hughes, *The Sociological Eye,* 3 vols. (Chicago, 1971); W. J. Goode, "Encroachment, Charlatanism, and the Emerging Profession," *American Sociological Review* (December 1960); and Robert K. Merton, "Some Thoughts on the Professions in American Society," Brown University Papers, XXXVII, 1960.

32. The contemporary discussion of what is called "human capital" was largely launched by Theodore Schultz's presidential address to the American Economic Association in 1960. See his "Investment in Human Capital," *American Economic Review* (March 1961), as well as his article on human capital in the *Encyclopedia of the Social Sciences* (New York, 1968), vol. 2. The most fundamental difficulty of Schultz's position is that it too readily assumes that higher incomes associated with higher education are due simply to the higher productivity of the more educated, an assumption I do not share, for reasons indicated by the discussion in note 31 above. The most important (if implicit) critique of that view is Randall Collins, "Functional and Conflict Theories of Educational Stratification," in J. Karabel and A. H. Halsey, eds., *Power and Ideology in Education* (New York, 1977). Collins argues that increased requirements for schooling are not due primarily to the greater skills required by jobs, or to the skills transmitted by education, but are mainly ways that competing status groups monopolize jobs by imposing their standards on personnel selection. Collins cites studies suggesting that some better educated workers are not necessarily more productive than those less educated. The main activity of schools, he holds, is to teach status cultures, thus socializing persons to gain admission to status groups and their privileges. Collins, however, acknowledges that "training in specific professions, such as medicine, engineering, scientific or scholarly research, teaching, and law can plausibly be considered vocationally relevant and possibly essential" (p. 1006). These, of course, are among the occupations central to the New Class. There is an important convergence between the main thrust of Collins' incisive work and Freidson's trenchant analysis of professions, though in a way Freidson is more "radical" in his critique of the professions. Both question the existence and significance of the special skills, techniques, or knowledge produced by advanced education. Despite Collins' disclaimer, the central thrust of his analysis is to question whether skill and *technical* knowledge is indeed produced by higher education, or whether it is needed. Couched in the framework of a *generalized* "conflict theory," educational requirements are held to reflect "the interests of whichever groups have power to set them," rather than job requirements. They are seen as a way of advancing the interests of specific status groups, who are engaged in a war of each against all for

wealth, prestige, and power. Cohesion is an important source of status groups' ability to win special privileges for themselves (by their struggles within organizations), and it is through the schools that status groups now increasingly acquire cohesion-building cultures. In a radically relativistic view, all status groups are seen as equally selfish, while none is regarded as actually contributing any more than others to the collective interest; the claim to do so would be seen as an *ideology* furthering that group's struggle for special privilege. There is, in short, *no* "universal class" in Collins' theory. In a demonic-Durkheimianism, all status groups are seen as equally vile. This also echoes Weber's pessimism, envisioning a conflict stiuation that can be resolved only by war. Yet Collins' theory also has a refreshing realism that escapes the Marxist mythification of the old proletariat as the "universal class." As my introduction to this essay makes plain, however, I reject the nihilism of Collins' generalized conflict theory in favor of a view of the New Class as a morally ambiguous, historically transient, but still "universal class." My reasons for doing so are outlined in thesis 14.1. For a recent and valuable discussion of education as legitimation that extends Collins' views, see John W. Meyer, "The Effect of Education as an Institution," *American Journal of Sociology* (July 1977). A basic source influencing my views of human capital is Irving Fisher, *The Nature of Capital and Income* (New York, 1927).

33. The critique of education as Collins develops it can remain a critique of that limited institutional sector (as it now tends to be), or it can develop into a general critique of capital in its various forms, as I here recommend.

34. For discussion of technology as a way of enhancing managerial control, rather than simply heightening productivity, see A. W. Gouldner, *Wildcat Strike* (Yellow Springs, 1954), especially p. 86.

35. See, for example, Gertrude Lenzer, ed., *Auguste Comte and Positivism, The Essential Writings* (New York, 1975), p. 399 ff.; and Ronald Fletcher, *Crisis of Industrial Civilization* (London, 1974), especially appendix, p. 246 ff.

36. See, for example, Schultz, "Investment in Human Capital"; for a critical appraisal of Schultz's calculation of the rates of return on investment in education, see Fritz Machlup, *The Production and Distribution of Knowledge*, p. 114.

37. Marx was normally disposed to focus on labor as "simple" labor not only as an analytic convenience but, in part also, because the "ends" to which labor were put under capitalism were not its own, so that culture-as-steering was invested elsewhere, in management; as, to culture-as-instruments such as skills and knowledge, Marx's emphasis was on their expropriation by capitalist management from the workers, through the growing division of labor and the development of technology. Since Marx sees workers as not establishing the ends of work *and* as losing such skills as they earlier had, a tacit *de-culturalization of labor* is premised in Marx. Thus Marx says, "for our purpose it suffices to consider only average labour, the costs of whose education and development are vanishing magnitudes." Marx then adds in a passing way that "I must seize upon this occasion to state that, as the costs of producing labouring powers of different quality do differ, so must the values of the labouring powers employed in different trades." The conclusion Marx draws from this is striking: "The cry for an *equality of wages* rests, therefore, upon a mistake, is an inane wish never to be fulfilled. . . . To clamour for *equal or even equitable retribution* on the basis of the wages system is the same as to clamour for *freedom* on the basis of the slavery system" (Karl Marx, *Value, Price and Profit* [New York, 1935], p. 39).

38. This section is indebted to Basil Bernstein and is based on a critical appropriation of his "elaborated and restricted linguistic codes," which have gone through various re-workings. That controversial classic was published in J. J. Gumperz and D. Hymes, *Directions in Sociolinguistics* (New York, 1972). A recent reworking is to be found in Bernstein's, "Social Class, Language, and Socialization," in T. A. Sebeok, ed., *Current Trends in Linguistics* (The Hague, 1974). For full bibliographic and other details see note 4 above.

39. Cf. Peter McHugh, "A Common-Sense Perception of Deviance," in H. P. Dreitzel, ed., *Recent Sociology, Number 2* (London, 1970), p. 165 ff. For good speech as "serious" speech see David Silverman, "Speaking Seriously," *Theory and Society* (Spring, 1974).

40. Bernstein's and Shils's work on the culture of intellectuals is importantly convergent, but is a convergence difficult to see because while Shils talks expressly about the culture of intellectuals, Bernstein's "elaborated code" is cast within the framework

of a sociolinguistics that has no special focus on intellectuals; it can be seen as convergent with Shils only after one concludes that it is not randomly distributed among social strata but is the special ideology of intellectuals. Bernstein's is essentially a linguistic translation of Shils's more conventional cultural analysis. Both also adopt "classicism" as their standpoint. This is fairly visible in Shils's lofty Goethian attitude toward Romanticism; for a discussion of the classical grounding of Bernstein's elaborated linguistic variant, see my *Dialectic of Ideology and Technology*, pp. 60–62.

41. See especially, Edward Shils, *The Intellectuals and the Powers and Other Essays* (Chicago, 1972).

42. Ibid., p. 7.

43. Ibid., p. 18.

44. Cf. Freidson, "The Futures of Professionalisation."

45. On the importance of censorship in the political formation of intellectuals, see A. W. Gouldner, *The Dialectic of Ideology and Technology*, pp. 102, 125–26.

46. For further development, see A. W. Gouldner, *The Coming Crisis of Western Sociology* (New York, 1970), especially, p. 151 ff.

47. Ibid., pp. 106, 153, 320.

48. Habermas stresses that technocratic consciousness and instrumental rationality entail a repression of ethics, thus undermining the requisites of practical reason and public politics. See, for example, J. Habermas, *Toward a Rational Society* (Boston, 1970), pp. 112–13. Clearly, in focussing on the "Legitimation Crisis" (Boston, 1975), Habermas has made the Weberian and Durkheimian problematics central to his own project. The most fundamental object of Habermas' work is to ground "critique" (as an alternative to positivist social science) *by establishing and justifying a system of moral norms*, which neither Marx nor the older generation of Critical theorists had done. Habermas' critique of Max Weber's value free doctrine, in the "Logic of Legitimation Problems," his work on socio-cultural evolution, and on the deduction of the characteristics of the ideal speech situation, are all centrally inspired by that goal, and thus he converges with Parsons' morality-centered sociology.

49. Chomsky, "Intellectuals and the State," p. 2.

50. Ibid., p. 10.

51. That is, there is a supposition that the group should be judged in

terms of the most sacred values, and not simply those of the everyday life applied to "ordinary" people. In a way, the resulting de-idealization is the obverse of the Parsonsian idealization of the professional.

52. Chomsky, "Intellectuals and the State," pp. 20–21.
53. Ibid., p. 26.
54. Ibid.
55. Robert Lilienfeld, *The Rise of Systems Theory* (New York, 1978), p. 263.
56. See Emile Durkheim, *Education and Sociology* (Glencoe, 1956); Louis Althusser, *Lenin and Philosophy and Other Essays* (London, 1971), especially the chapter on "Ideology and Ideological State Apparatuses"; and Herbert Marcuse, *One-Dimensional Man* (London, 1964). The continuity between Durkheim and Althusser, who regards schools as the dominant "ideological state apparatus," is striking, but not for the first time.
57. All quotations are from Howard R. Bowen, *Investment in Learning: The Individual and Social Value of American Higher Education* (San Francisco, 1977), p. 73.
58. Ibid.
59. Ibid., p. 77.
60. Ibid., p. 78 ff.
61. Ibid., pp. 125–26.
62. Ibid., pp. 94–95.
63. Ibid., pp. 116–17.
64. Thomas S. Kuhn, *The Structure of Scientific Revolutions* (Chicago, 1970) second edition, enlarged.
65. See Khalil Nakhleh, "Palestinian Dilemma: Nationalist Consciousness and University Education" (ms., 1976).
66. For fuller discussion of the differences and contradictions between bureaucrats and technical intelligentsia, see my *Dialectic of Ideology and Technology*, p. 266 ff.
67. As a consequence, when technical intelligentsia are monitored by organizational superiors, "it is results that count" for it is often only these that *can* be judged.
68. The testimony on this is venerable: in Plato's *Republic*, Socrates proposes to defer training in the dialectic until students are in their thirties and have passed other tests. And then, he warns, great caution is needed:
    "Why great caution?"
    "Do you not remark," I said, "how great is the evil which dialectic has introduced?"

"What evil?" he said.

"The students of the art are filled with lawlessness" (*Republic*, 437 DE). For fuller discussion see my *Enter Plato* (New York, 1965), p. 279. In short, the dialectic, like CCD, has certain inherent costs which Nietzsche was among the first to notice. Thus CCD cannot simply be equated with "good" speech.

69. As note 37 above indicates, this is no less true for the Marxist contingent of the New Class than of others. Equality has never been a high priority value for Marxism.

70. While editing this, a recent people's congress in Peking eliminated the cultural revolution's "revolutionary committees" in factories and schools, began to refurbish wage differentials, and recharged higher education, the essential reproductive mechanism of the New Class.

71. Louis Althusser's argument, that Stalinism was a fumbled attack on the New Class, has many difficulties. Not least is the fact that among the delegates to the 18th Congress of the CPSU in 1939, two years after the purges, about 26% had higher education, compared to the 10% with higher education among delegates of the 17th Congress in 1934, who were a central target of Stalin's terror. For further discussion, see A. W. Gouldner, "Stalinism," *Telos* (Winter 1977–78).

72. K. S. Karol, *Guerrillas in Power* (New York, 1970), p. 401.

73. For documentation of this and of the extraordinarily high educational level of the early revolutionary leaders in the USSR and Vietnam, see my "Prologue to a Theory of Revolutionary Intellectuals," *Telos* (Winter 1975–76).

74. Christine Pelzer White, in J. W. Lewis, ed., *Peasant Rebellion and Communist Revolution in Asia* (Stanford, 1974).

75. Cf. William Shawcross, "Cambodia Under Its New Rulers," *New York Review of Books* (March 4, 1976).

76. Goran Therborn, *Science, Class and Society* (London, 1976); see especially p. 317 ff.

77. "The Roles of the Intellectual and Political Roles," in A. Gella, ed., *The Intelligentsia and the Intellectuals* (Beverly Hills, 1976), pp. 112–13.

78. Karl Marx and Friedrich Engels, *The German Ideology* (New York, n.d.), p. 69.

79. *Communist Manifesto*, p. 26.

80. Cf. Sartre: "What he [Stalin] hated about Trotsky was not so much the measures he proposed as the whole praxis in the name of which he proposed them" (Jean-Paul Sartre, "Socialism in

One Country," *New Left Review* [November–January 1977], p. 146). For my own more extended statement on the relationship between Trotskyism and Stalinism, see A. W. Gouldner, "Stalinism," *Telos* (Winter 1977–78), pp. 22–26.

81. On Jacobins as blocked ascendents, see the good discussion by Lewis A. Coser, *Men of Ideas* (New York, 1970): "As one moved, then, from the rank and file of the Jacobins to the leadership of the various societies, the proportion of intellectuals increased. And if one moved from provincial leadership groups to the men who enacted key political roles . . . intellectuals become predominant. . . . If we consider the very top group, those twelve men who constituted the Committee of Public Safety during the terror, we encountered only intellectuals" (pp. 146–47). Coser develops the argument that the Jacobin leadership was composed largely of those whose careers had manifested upward mobility but whose future ascendence was blocked. The study of diverse career blockages—e.g., of educated clerkly revolutionaries, of the sons of those killed during nationalist struggles, of displaced elites—is crucial to an understanding of the radicalization of intellectuals. A basic and familiar source of such a blockage is, of course, having the "wrong" gender, ethnic, national, racial, linguistic, or religious identity. Thus early communist leadership in Czarist Russia had a "relatively high proportion of men of non-Russian extraction," according to W. E. Mosse, *Slavonic and East European Review* (1968), p. 151. Radicalized Jews are thus simply a special case of this more general problem of blocked ascendence. But we need to be careful not to overestimate the role of injured material interests in producing radicalization nor underestimate injured ideal interests (in CCD) which, when offended, can also radicalize. And it is not only career blockages which may sharpen radicalization (e.g., Marx), but *prior* radicalization may elicit repressive career blockages which only then further intensify the preblockage radicalization (again Marx).

82. See E. Shils, "The Intellectual in the Political Development of the New States," *World Politics* (XII, 1960), pp. 329–68. Cf. Also C. W. Mills: "Brought into being by the schools of Western nations, they are often condemned to a *declassé* kind of existence . . . an intellectual proletariat which can find no suitable place among the illiterate masses, among the beginnings of the middle classes or in such alien organizations of Western business

or government agencies as may exist. . . . Given their situation
they have tended to reject the capitalism of the West" (C. W.
Mills, *Power, Politics and People* [New York, n.d.], pp. 413–14).
Of course, mere admission to such a school was already a promise, and for many the experience, of an upward mobility that
generated expectations that subsequently went unfulfilled; thus,
"blocked ascendence."

83. See Paul Cocks et al., eds., *Dynamics of Soviet Politics* (Cambridge, 1976).

84. The citation from Alexander Gella in the previous paragraph is
Gella, ed., *The Intelligentsia and the Intellectuals*, p. 29. The ci-
tation bearing on the American revolution is from James Kirby
Martin, *Men in Rebellion* (New York, 1973), p. 138.

85. Ibid., p. 173.

86. Charles Kadushin et al.; see note 27 above.

87. For these remarkable letters, in which, among other things,
Comte complains that men of business offend the theoretical
dignity of intellectuals, see Frank Manuel, *The New World of
Henri Saint-Simon* (Cambridge, 1956)

88. *New Republic* (January 14, 1931).

89. Cf. Sebastian de Grazia, *The Political Community: A Study of
Anomie* (Chicago, 1948).

90. The studies mentioned above are ably summarized in David N.
Smith, *Who Rules the Universities*, p. 253 ff. The studies reported below, which develop the details, are all from the official
publication of the United States Bureau of Labor Statistics, *Occupational Outlook;* specific citations are given in the text.

91. In J. Foster and D. Long, eds., *Protest: Student Activism in
America* (New York, 1970), p. 137.

92. See Kenneth Keniston, *Young Radicals* (New York, 1968):
". . . many activists are concerned about living out expressed
but unimplemented parental values . . . many demonstrators
are 'acting out' in their demonstrations the values that their
parents explicitly believed . . ." (p. 309). Relative to my central
thesis, however, the most basic point Keniston makes is that "activists are not drawn from disadvantaged, status-anxious, under-
privileged, or uneducated groups; on the contrary, they are
selectively recruited from among those young Americans who have
had the most socially fortunate upbringings" (p. 307). And relevant to the point made in the text below, concerning the special
activist role of student assistants: "The most effective protest

leaders have not been undergraduates, but teaching assistants. The presence of large numbers of exploited, underpaid, disgruntled, and frustrated teacher assistants (or other equivalent graduate students and younger faculty members) is essential for organized and persistent protest" (p. 312).

93. For fuller development of my argument, see A. W. Gouldner, "Marxism and Social Theory," *Theory and Society* (1, 1974).

94. Thus when Marx and Engels upbraided Wilhelm Weitling, then one of the German revolutionary leaders of working class origin, they denounced him above all for his lack of "theory," calling him an abject fraud because of this deficiency. Marx also distrusted the autodidacts among the workers, claiming that when they "give up work and become professional literary men, [they] always set some theoretical mischief going . . ." (Letter to Sorge, London, October 19, 1877).

95. The destruction of the CPSU under Stalinism is discussed in my "Stalinism," *Telos* (Winter 1977–78).

96. Scholarship in Gramsci is a thriving industry these days. A few of the better items: Paul Piccone, "Gramsci's Marxism: Beyond Leninism and Togliatti," *Theory and Society* (Winter 1976); Jerome Karabel, "Revolutionary Contradictions: Antonio Gramsci and the Problem of Intellectuals," *Politics and Society* (6, 1976); Carl Boggs, *Gramsci's Marxism* (New York, 1976).

97. See Albert Parry, *The New Class Divided* (New York, 1966).

98. *Foreign Policy* (Winter 1974–75), p. 118.

99. For detailed discussion of this debt, see Ellen Brun and Jacques Hersh, "Paradoxes in the Political Economy of Détente," *Theory and Society* (May 1978).

100. See Alexander Yanov, *Détente After Brezhnev* (Berkeley, 1972).

# INDEX OF SUBJECTS